PATCHWORK
for Your Home

Betty Deane Eastham

ONDORI

CONTENTS

★ Copyright © 1984 Ondorisha Publishers Ltd., All Rights Reserved.
★ Published by Ondorisha Publishers Ltd.,
  32 Nishigoken-cho, Shinjuku-ku, Tokyo 162, Japan.
★ Sole Overseas Distributor: Japan Publications Trading Co., Ltd.
  P.O. Box 5030 Tokyo International, Tokyo, Japan.
★ Distributed in the United States by Kodansha International/USA Ltd. through Harper & Row,
  Publishers, Inc., 10 East 53rd Street, New York, New York 10022.

10 9 8 7 6 5 4 3 2 1

ISBN 0-87040-585-3
Printed in Japan

CLASSIC PATCHWORK

EIGHT-POINTED STAR TABLECLOTH

Instructions on page 2.

Fabrics Used (Actual Size)

ⓐ   ⓑ   ⓒ   ⓓ   ⓔ   ⓕ

Eight-pointed Star Tablecloth,
shown on page 1.

MATERIALS
FABRICS: (a) 90cm by 135cm; (b) 90cm by 70cm; (c)-(f) 40cm by 25cm each; cotton fabric for lining, 123cm by 98cm. Thin quilt batting, 98cm by 123cm. White and dark brown quilting thread.

FINISHED SIZE: 123cm by 98cm.

DIRECTIONS:
1. Cut out patches and sew them together by hand. Make 6 blocks. Then assemble blocks with borders.
2. Transfer quilting patterns to borders. Draw diamond patterns, moving template as indicated.
3. Pin and baste top, batting and lining together. Quilt along quilting lines, starting from center toward each side.
4. Bind edges to finish.

Cutting

Top See next page for eight-pointed star patterns.
Add 0.7cm seam allowance all around unless otherwise indicated.

Quilt batting   123cm × 98cm

Lining (cotton fabric)   123cm × 98cm

No seam allowance along edges to be bound.

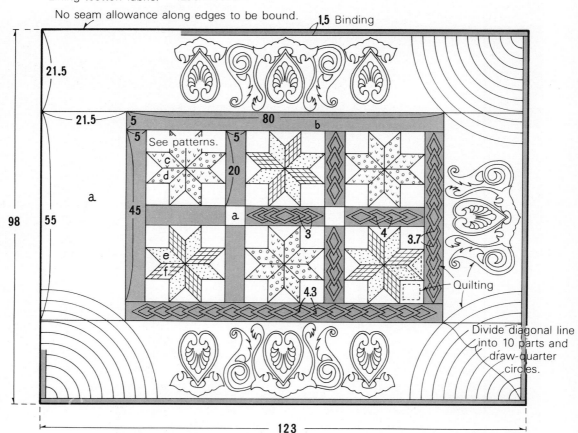

1.5 Binding

21.5

21.5   5
5   80   b
See patterns.
c
d   5   20
a   45   a   3   4   3.7
e   55   4.3
f
98   Quilting
Divide diagonal line into 10 parts and draw quarter circles.

123

Corner

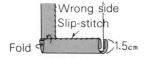

Wrong side
Slip-stitch
Fold   1.5cm

Strip for binding

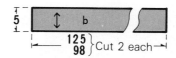

5   b
125
98   Cut 2 each

2

Patterns for Eight-pointed Star Block (Actual size) Add 0.7 cm seam allowance.

Quilt with white quilting thread

a Cut 24 pieces

a Cut 24 pieces

c ~ f
Cut 12 pieces each

Quilting patterns
(Actual size)

Quilt with
dark brown thread.

Center

Quilt with
white quilting thread.

Quilting Pattern for Side.

3

FAN TABLECLOTH
Instructions on page 6.

ⓐ

ⓑ

ⓒ

ⓓ

ⓔ

ⓕ

ⓖ

ⓗ

ⓘ

MATERIALS

FABRICS: (a)-(f) silk crepe, 50cm by 15cm; (g) silk crepe, 15cm square; (h) for lining, 1m by 2m; (i) for binding, 90cm by 20cm. Quilt batting, 1m square. White and black quilting thread.

FINISHED SIZE: 1m square.

DIRECTIONS:

1. Cut out patches for fans. Sew 6 patches together by hand.
2. Appliqué pieced fans in place with slip stitch.
3. Transfer quilting patterns.
4. Pin and baste top, batting and lining together. Quilt along quilting lines, starting from center outward. Embroider ribs of fans in chain stitch.
5. Bind edges to finish.

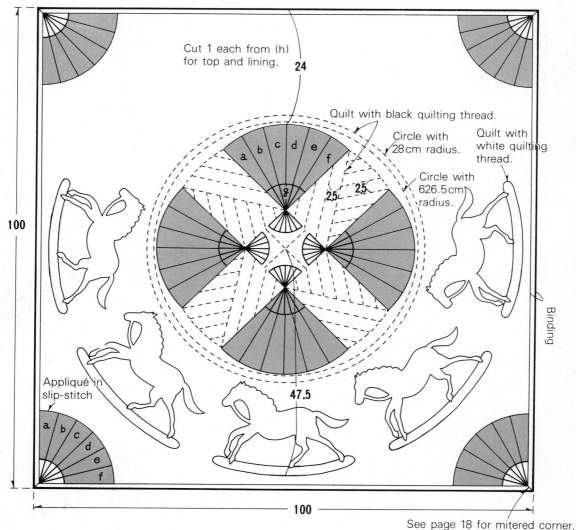

Cut 1 each from (h) for top and lining.

24

Quilt with black quilting thread.

Circle with 28cm radius.

Quilt with white quilting thread.

Circle with 626.5cm radius.

a b c d e f

g

25 25

100

Appliqué in slip-stitch

a b c d e f

47.5

100

Binding

See page 18 for mitered corner.

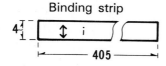

Binding strip

4

i

405

6

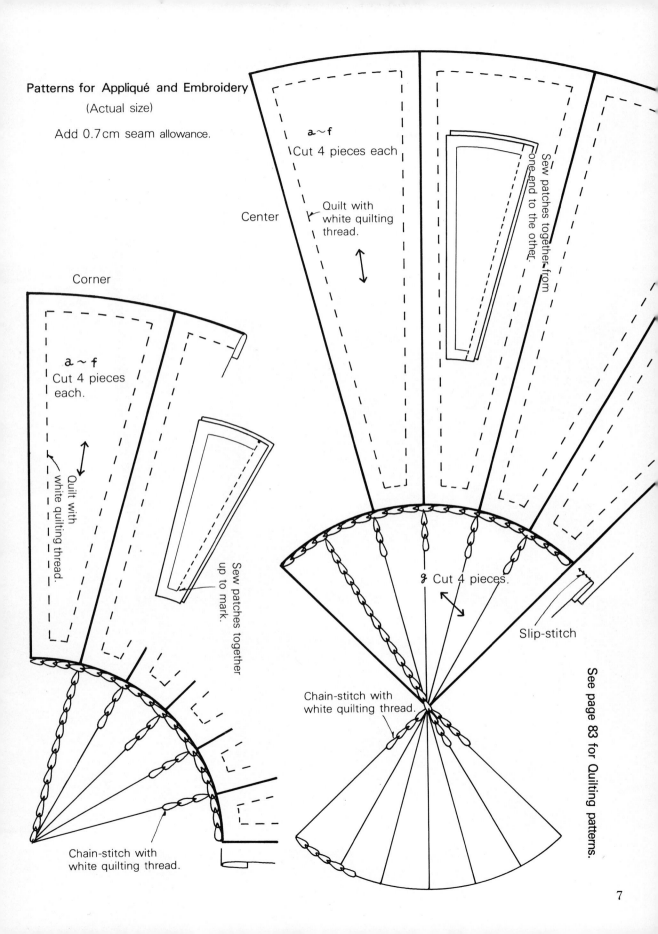

Patterns for Appliqué and Embroidery

(Actual size)

Add 0.7cm seam allowance.

a ~ f
Cut 4 pieces each

Center

Quilt with white quilting thread.

Sew patches together from one end to the other.

Corner

a ~ f
Cut 4 pieces each.

Quilt with white quilting thread.

Sew patches together up to mark.

ℊ Cut 4 pieces.

Slip-stitch

Chain-stitch with white quilting thread.

Chain-stitch with white quilting thread.

See page 83 for Quilting patterns.

7

Fabrics Used (Actual Size)

a   b   c   d   e   f   g

**Fabrics Used
(Actual Size)**

PILLOWS

Instructions on page 10.

MATERIALS

FABRICS FOR LEFT PILLOW: (a) 75 cm by 46 cm; (b) 33 cm square; (c, d, e, f) 17 cm square each; (g) 24 cm by 16 cm; for lining (a) 45 cm square.

FABRICS FOR RIGHT PILLOW: (2) 80 cm by 46 cm; (1) 90 cm by 20 cm; (3-38) small amount each of 36 different prints; for lining (1) 45 cm square. Quilt batting, 45 cm square. Quilting thread: white for left pillow and white & black for right pillow. 35 cm zipper. 45 cm-square inner pillow stuffed with kapok.

FINISHED SIZE: 43.5 cm square.

DIRECTIONS:

1. Cut out patches and sew them together by hand.
2. Pin and baste top, batting and lining together. Quilt.
3. Sew zipper onto back piece with 2 cm seams.
4. With right sides facing, sew front and back pieces together and zigzag-stitch along raw edges by machine. Turn inside out.
5. Insert inner pillow.

Left pillow

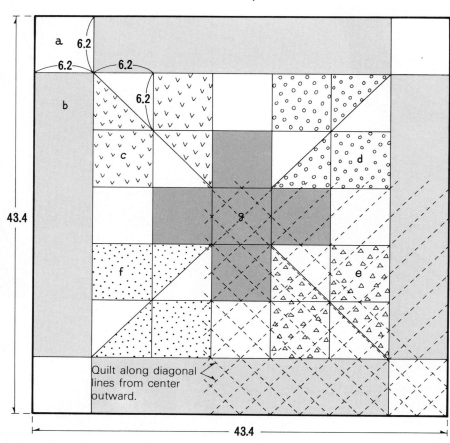

Cutting

Top
Front Add 0.7 cm seam allowance.

	6.2 cm square	6.2 cm triangle
a	8 pieces	8 pieces
c	2 "	2 "
d	2 "	2 "
e	2 "	2 "
f	2 "	2 "
g	5 pieces	
b	6.2 cm × 31 cm 4 pieces	

Cut batting and lining 45 cm square each.

Cut 2 pieces from (a) for back, 46 cm by 25 cm each.

Quilt along diagonal lines from center outward.

43.4

43.4

Piecing

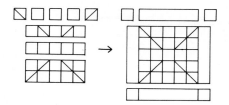

Right pillow

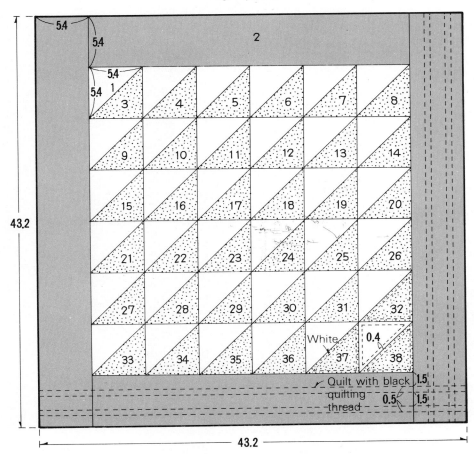

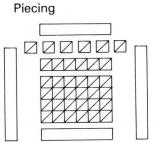

Cutting

Front

Top Add 0.7cm seam allowance.

2	5.4cm × 32.4cm	2 pieces
	5.4cm × 43.2cm	2 pieces
1	5.4cm triangle	36 pieces
3~38	〃	1 piece each

Cut batting and lining 45cm square each.

Cut 2 pieces from (2) for back,
45cm by 25cm each.

Piecing

GRANDMA'S FLOWER GARDEN TABLECLOTH

Instructions on page 14.

Fabrics Used (Actual Size)

MATERIALS

FABRICS: (a) at least 90 cm by 130 cm (required amount of fabric differs depending on designs); (b) 90 cm by 270 cm; (c) 90 cm by 170 cm; (d) for underlay, 90 cm by 6 m; for lining, 90 cm by 360 cm.

FINISHED SIZE: 176 cm in diameter. (Diameter of underlay is 226 cm.)

DIRECTIONS:

1. Cut out patches and sew them together as shown in diagram. After piecing all patches, cut off excess beyond circle rim.
2. Join pieces for lining. Cut out lining same size as top. With wrong sides together, apply glue between layers in several places.
3. Bind edges with bias-cut strips, showing 1.5 cm binding on front.
4. Cut out fabric for underlay and sew 3 pieces together. Bind edges to finish.

Sew pieces for lining together and then cut out same size as top.

Cut off excess after piecing.

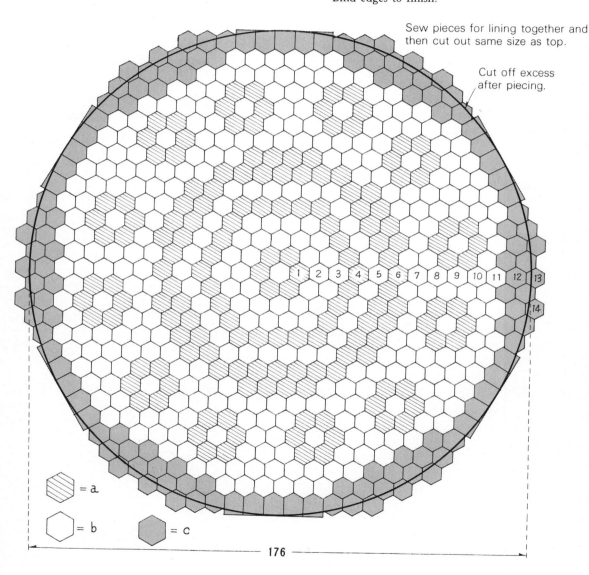

= a

= b

= c

176

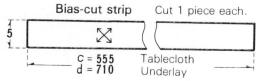

Bias-cut strip   Cut 1 piece each.

5

c = 555   Tablecloth
d = 710   Underlay

14

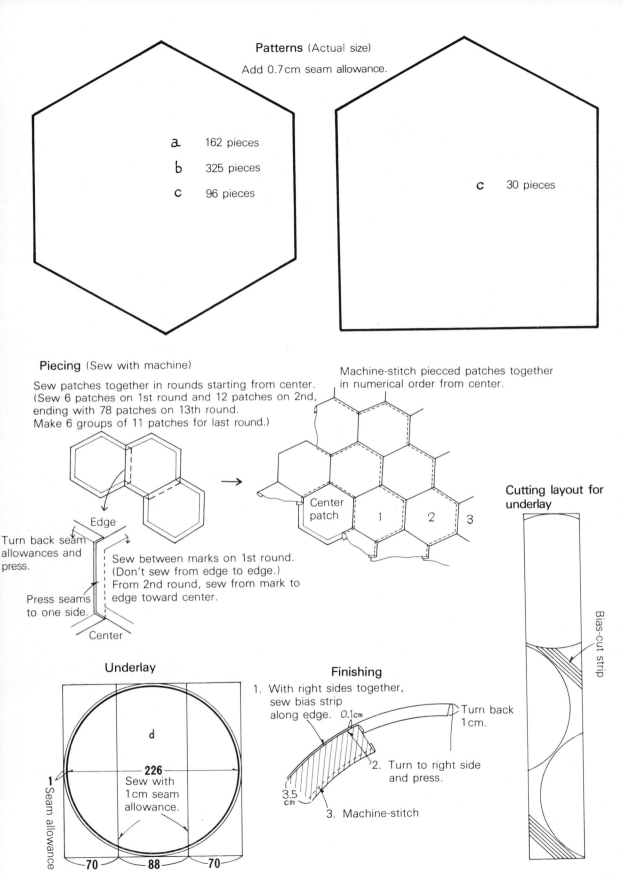

Patterns (Actual size)

Add 0.7 cm seam allowance.

a   162 pieces

b   325 pieces

c   96 pieces

c   30 pieces

Piecing (Sew with machine)

Sew patches together in rounds starting from center.
(Sew 6 patches on 1st round and 12 patches on 2nd,
ending with 78 patches on 13th round.
Make 6 groups of 11 patches for last round.)

Machine-stitch piecced patches together
in numerical order from center.

Edge

Turn back seam
allowances and
press.

Sew between marks on 1st round.
(Don't sew from edge to edge.)
From 2nd round, sew from mark to
edge toward center.

Press seams
to one side.

Center

Center
patch   1   2   3

Cutting layout for underlay

Bias-cut strip

Underlay

d

226
Sew with
1 cm seam
allowance.

1
Seam allowance

70   **88**   **70**

Finishing

1. With right sides together,
   sew bias strip
   along edge.   0.1cm   Turn back
   1 cm.

2. Turn to right side
   and press.

3.5
cm

3. Machine-stitch

15

d

c

b

a

Blue Pillow

YO-YO FLOWER PILLOWS
Instructions on page 18.

e

f

g

h

i

j

k

l

m

16

Orange Pillow

(a)

(b)

(c)

(d)

(e)

(f)

(g)

(h)

(i)

(j)

(k)

(l)

(m)

17

Yo-yo Flower Pillows,
shown on pages 16 & 17.

MATERIALS

FABRICS: (a) 90 cm by 42 cm; (f, h, i) 22 cm by 16 cm each; (b, c, d, e, g, j, k, l, m) 20 cm square each; for lining, 42 cm square. Quilt batting, 42 cm square. Six-strand embroidery floss, No. 25; 1/2 skein each of dark and light olive green. White quilting thread. 33 cm zipper. Polyester fiberfill. 42 cm-square inner pillow stuffed with kapok.

FINISHED SIZE: 42 cm square.

DIRECTIONS:

1. Cut out patches for planter and two buds. Sew patches together using cardboard and whip stitch (see page 125). Make flowers following diagrams.

2. Enlarge quilting patterns and transfer to front piece. Mark places for appliques.

3. Appliqué planter with slip stitch and work running stitches along seams of each hexagon.

4. Pin and baste front, batting and lining together. Quilt.

5. Embroider stems. Sew on flowers. Appliqué buds padded with polyester fiberfill using slip stitch.

6. Sew zipper onto back pieces. With wrong sides facing, bind edges of front and back pieces together.

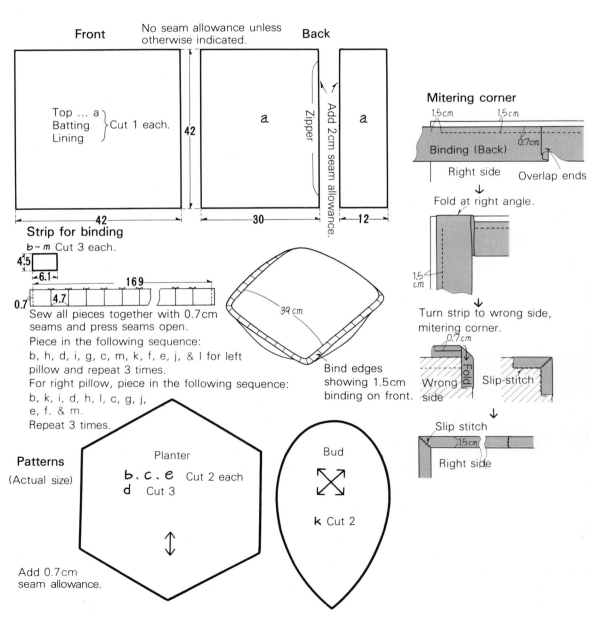

No seam allowance unless otherwise indicated.

Front

Top ... a
Batting
Lining } Cut 1 each.

42

42

Back

a

Zipper

Add 2cm seam allowance.

a

30

12

Strip for binding

b ~ m Cut 3 each.

4.5
6.1
4.7
0.7
169

Sew all pieces together with 0.7 cm seams and press seams open.

Piece in the following sequence:

b, h, d, i, g, c, m, k, f, e, j, & l for left pillow and repeat 3 times.

For right pillow, piece in the following sequence:

b, k, i, d, h, l, c, g, j, e, f, & m.

Repeat 3 times.

39 cm

Bind edges showing 1.5 cm binding on front.

Mitering corner

1.5 cm   1.5 cm
0.7 cm
Binding (Back)
Right side   Overlap ends

Fold at right angle.

1.5 cm

Turn strip to wrong side, mitering corner.

0.7 cm
Fold   Slip-stitch
Wrong side

Slip stitch
1.5 cm
Right side

Patterns

(Actual size)

Planter

b, c, e Cut 2 each
d Cut 3

Add 0.7 cm seam allowance.

Bud

k Cut 2

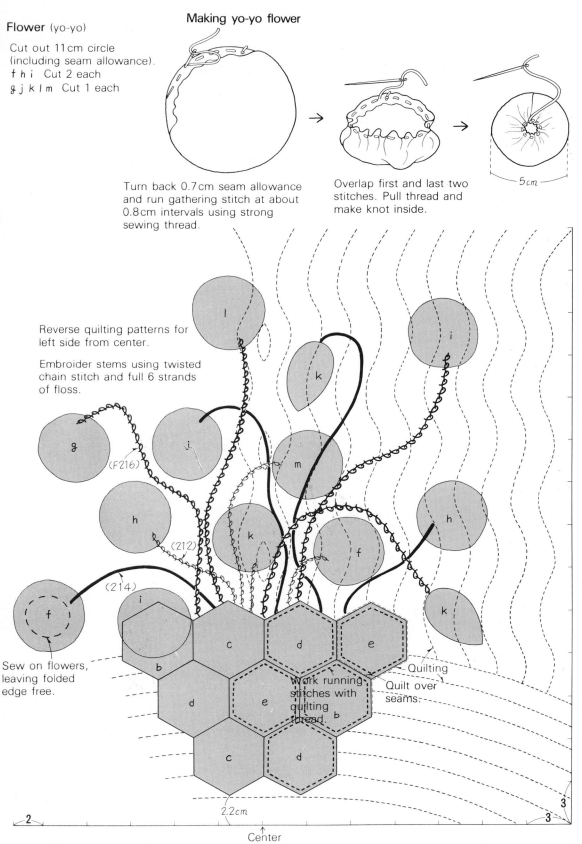

Flower (yo-yo)

Cut out 11cm circle
(including seam allowance).
f h i Cut 2 each
g j k l m Cut 1 each

Making yo-yo flower

Turn back 0.7cm seam allowance
and run gathering stitch at about
0.8cm intervals using strong
sewing thread.

Overlap first and last two
stitches. Pull thread and
make knot inside.

5cm

Reverse quilting patterns for
left side from center.

Embroider stems using twisted
chain stitch and full 6 strands
of floss.

(F216)

(212)

(214)

Sew on flowers,
leaving folded
edge free.

Work running
stitches with
quilting
thread.

Quilting

Quilt over
seams.

2.2cm

2

3

3

Center

19

PINK BOW CRIB QUILT

Instructions on page 22.

Fabrics Used (Actual Size)

ⓐ

ⓑ

ⓒ

ⓓ

ⓔ

21

Pink Bow Crib Quilt,
shown on pages 20 & 21.

MATERIALS
FABRICS: (a) 90 cm square; (b, c) 90 cm by 45 cm each; (d) 60 cm by 30 cm; (e) 62 cm square; for lining and backing, 104 cm square each. Quilt batting, 104 cm square. DMC Six-strand embroidery floss, No. 25: 1-1/2 skeins each of pink (963), peacock-green (993) and blue (3325); 1 skein each of peacock-green (992) and olive-green (988); 1/2 skein each of peony-rose (602), rose pink (309), pink (225), blue (312), purple (552), brown (975) and white; small amount each of rose-pink (335), peacock-blue (806, 824), purple (209) and dark brown (898).

FINISHED SIZE: 104 cm square.
DIRECTIONS:
1. Cut out patches and appliques. Appliqué as indicated using slip stitch.
2. Transfer enlarged quilting patterns onto fabric (e).
3. Sew patches together by machine.
4. Pin and baste top, batting and backing together. Quilt center design, patches and outlines of appliques.
5. Place quilted piece on lining and bind edges to finish.

Quilting patterns Quilt with 4 strands of floss and back-stitch unless otherwise indicated.

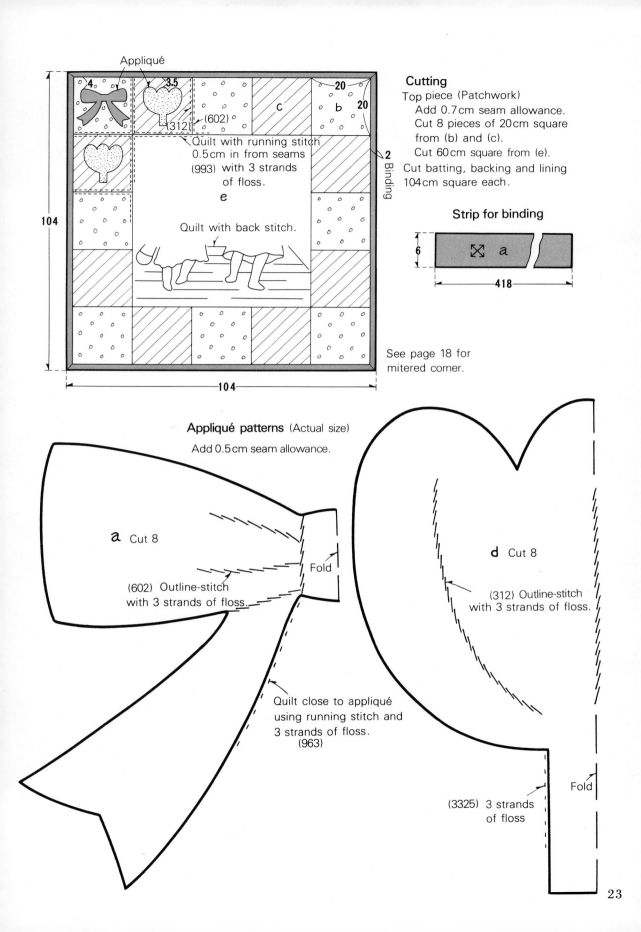

Cutting

Top piece (Patchwork)

Add 0.7 cm seam allowance.

Cut 8 pieces of 20 cm square from (b) and (c).

Cut 60 cm square from (e).

Cut batting, backing and lining 104 cm square each.

Strip for binding

See page 18 for mitered corner.

Appliqué

Quilt with running stitch 0.5 cm in from seams (993) with 3 strands of floss.

Quilt with back stitch.

Appliqué patterns (Actual size)

Add 0.5 cm seam allowance.

a Cut 8

(602) Outline-stitch with 3 strands of floss.

Quilt close to appliqué using running stitch and 3 strands of floss. (963)

d Cut 8

(312) Outline-stitch with 3 strands of floss.

(3325) 3 strands of floss

Fold

23

e

f

g

h

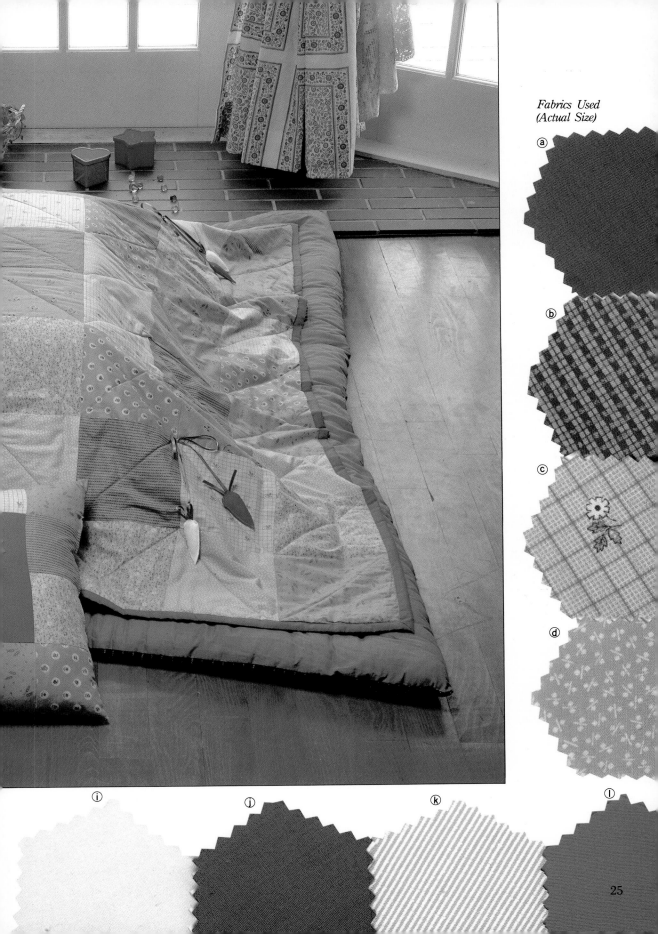

Fabrics Used
(Actual Size)

ⓐ

ⓑ

ⓒ

ⓓ

ⓘ

ⓙ

ⓚ

ⓛ

25

TABLECLOTH
MATERIALS

FABRICS: (a) 91cm by 362cm; (e, f) 84cm square each; (b, c, d, g, h) 84cm by 63cm each. Quilt batting, 120cm by 350cm. Olive green sewing thread, No. 30. White and vermilion felt, 20cm square each. Olive green ribbon, 0.5cm wide and 5.2m long. Polyester fiberfill.
FINISHED SIZE: 175cm square.

DIRECTIONS:

1. Cut out patches and sew them together by machine.
2. Join pieces of batting (see page 125). Join pieces of lining.
3. Pin and baste top, batting and lining together. Quilt by machine.
4. Turn lining over top, turn in seam allowances and machine-stitch.
5. Make radishes and carrots with felt and sew in place.

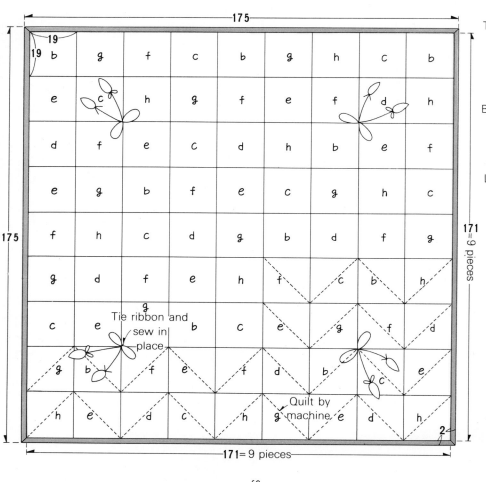

Cutting

Top Cut patches 21cm square.

bd = 10 pieces each
h = 11 pieces
cg = 12 pieces each
ef = 13 pieces each

Batting Sew 2 pieces of 120cm by 175cm together and cut into 175cm square.

Lining Cut out 2 pieces of 91cm by 181cm from (a) and sew them together with 0.5cm seams to make 181cm square.

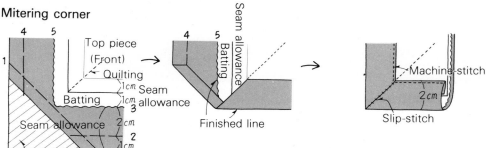

Mitering corner

Top piece (Front)
Quilting
Seam allowance
Batting
Seam allowance
Finished line
Machine-stitch
Slip-stitch
Seam allowance
Cut out lining.
Fold in numerical order.

Patterns for Carrot and Radish

(Actual size)

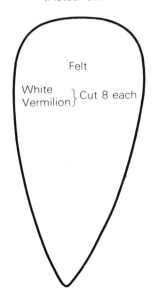

Felt

White
Vermilion } Cut 8 each

How to make carrot and radish

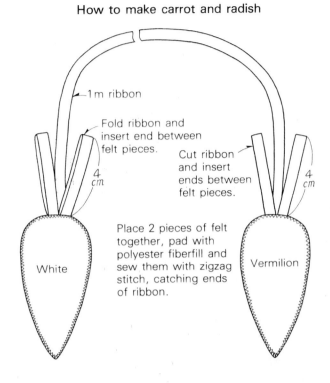

—1 m ribbon

Fold ribbon and
insert end between
felt pieces.

4 cm

Cut ribbon
and insert
ends between
felt pieces.

4 cm

Place 2 pieces of felt
together, pad with
polyester fiberfill and
sew them with zigzag
stitch, catching ends
of ribbon.

White

Vermilion

PILLOW
MATERIALS
FABRICS FOR RADISH: (a) 73 cm by 48 cm; (b, c, d, e, g) 27 cm by 14 cm each; (f, h) 14 cm square each; (i) 11 cm by 5 cm; (j) 10 cm square.
FOR CARROT: (a) 73 cm by 48 cm; (c, e, f, g, h) 27 cm by 14 cm each; (b, d) 14 cm square each; (k) 9 cm by 5 cm; (l) 17 cm square. Six-strand embroidery floss, No. 25: white and dark green for radish; red and green for carrot. 30 cm zipper. 48 cm-square inner pillow stuffed with kapok. Polyester fiberfill.
FINISHED SIZE: 46 cm square.
DIRECTIONS:
1. Cut out patches and sew them together by machine.
2. Appliqué and embroider in place.
3. Sew on zipper. With right sides facing, sew front and back pieces together. Turn inside out.
4. Insert inner pillow.

Cutting
Front (patchwork)   Add 1 cm seam allowance.
Back   Cut 48 cm square from (a).

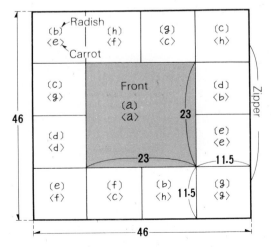

See page 84 for Appliqué patterns.

Patchwork Gifts

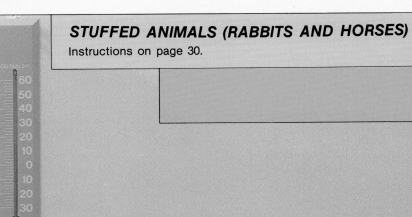

HOUSE WALL HANGING

Instructions on page 85.

STUFFED ANIMALS (RABBITS AND HORSES)

Instructions on page 30.

MATERIALS
FOR BIG HORSE
FABRIC: Cotton fabric: (a) 50 cm by 30 cm; (b-g) Small amount of each. Polyester fiberfill. Six-strand embroidery floss, No. 25: Beige and yellow. Beige looped yarn. Scrap of light brown felt. 2 black beads.

FOR SMALL HORSE
FABRIC: Unbleached sheeting, 45 cm by 20 cm; cotton broadcloth, small amount each of red and red with white dots. Red embroidery floss, No. 25. 1 skein of basting thread. Scrap of red felt. Polyester fiberfill. 8 gold beads, 0.6 cm in diameter; 2 black beads.

FOR RABBIT
FABRIC: Cotton fabric: FOR GREEN RABBIT: (a) 40 cm square; (b-e) small amount each. FOR BLUE RABBIT: Blue, 20 cm by 15 cm; small amount each of 11 different prints. FOR RED RABBIT: Red, 32 cm by 18 cm; small amount each of red with white dots and red with floral design. 3 black beads for each. Black sewing thread. Six-strand embroidery floss, No. 25: Small amount each of red and white. Red pencil.
FINISHED SIZE: See diagram for HORSE. GREEN RABBIT, 28 cm tall. BLUE AND RED RABBITS, 16 cm tall.
DIRECTIONS:
Cut out patches adding 0.5 cm seam allowance. Sew them together by machine.
FOR HORSE: Follow directions below.
FOR RABBITS: Make in same manner as HORSE. Make features.

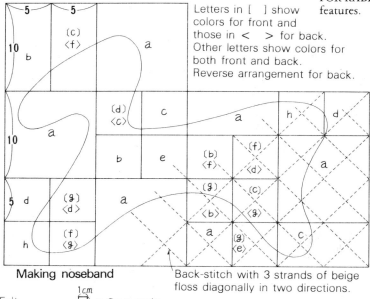

Letters in [ ] show colors for front and those in < > for back. Other letters show colors for both front and back. Reverse arrangement for back.

Making noseband

Back-stitch with 3 strands of beige floss diagonally in two directions.

After piecing patches and finishing embroidery, cut out pattern adding 1 cm seam allowance.

Pattern

With right sides of front and back together, stitch all around twice, leaving opening for turning. Trim excess 0.7 cm beyond seams and clip into curves. Turn inside out. Stuff with polyester fiberfill and slip-stitch opening closed.

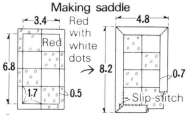

Making saddle

Sew patches together with 0.5 cm seams.

Cut 7.2 cm by 10.6 cm from red for lining. Turn edges of lining over top, turn in seam allowances and slip-stitch (see page 26).

Felt
Sew end onto inside ring
Sew ends to make ring
10 cm (6 cm)
Slip-stitch
12 cm (8 cm)
1 cm

( ) shows required length for SMALL HORSE.

Cut one side.
Cardboard
5 cm
Wind looped yarn around cardboard.
Sew looped yarn onto seams of head with back stitch.
Trim mane.

Sew on beads on both sides, pull thread tightly and make knot.

2 cm 7 cm
Wind yellow embroidery floss.

25 cm Noseband

32 cm

Slip-stitch saddle
5 cm
2 cm
Wind with red embroidery floss.

16 cm
Sew on beads.
16 cm

Cut strands of basting thread into 5 cm pieces, place center of threads on seams of head and sew with back stitch.

GREEN RABBIT Use fabric (a) for back.

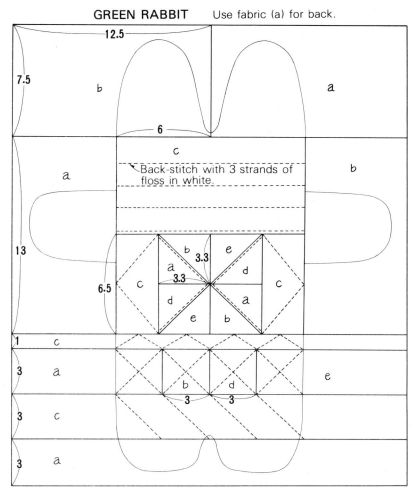

12.5

7.5

b

a

6

c

← Back-stitch with 3 strands of floss in white.

a

b

13

b 3.3 e

a d

6.5 c 3.3 c

d a

e b

1 c

3 a

b d

3 3

3 c

3 a

e

BLUE RABBIT Use blue for back.

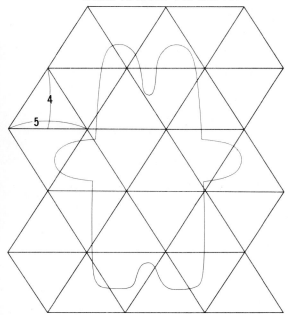

4

5

RED RABBIT Use red for back.

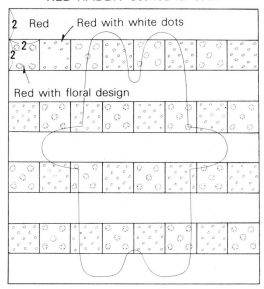

2 Red   Red with white dots

2
2

Red with floral design

See page 87 for actual-size patterns.

X'MAS ORNAMENTS

Instructions for Pillows on page 91, for Wreath on page 34
and for other ornaments on page 114.

Wreath with Snowman,
shown on pages 32 & 33.

MATERIALS

FABRICS: Cotton fabric: (a) red with white dots, 50 cm by 15 cm; (b) print with large holly leaves, (c) red with design, 35 cm by 25 cm each; (d) print with small holly leaves 35 cm square; (e) red, 45 cm square. Green satin: 60 cm by 50 cm. Scrap of striped cotton for muffler. Six-strand embroidery floss, No. 25: White, gray, red and dark brown. Scraps of white and black felt. Red ribbon, 1.2 cm by 20 cm. Polyester fiberfill, 300 g. Black felt-tip pen.
FINISHED SIZE: 39 cm in diameter.

DIRECTIONS:
1. Cut out patches adding seam allowances. Sew them together by hand starting from center. Embroider.
2. Sew front and back together with right sides facing outside edge. Turn inside out.
3. Fold front seam allowance to back seam allowance of inside edge, and slip-stitch finely leaving opening for stuffing. Stuff with fiberfill tightly, and slip-stitch opening closed.
4. Sew loop for hanging onto back.
5. Tie ribbon into bow and sew on front.
6. Make snowman and attach in place.

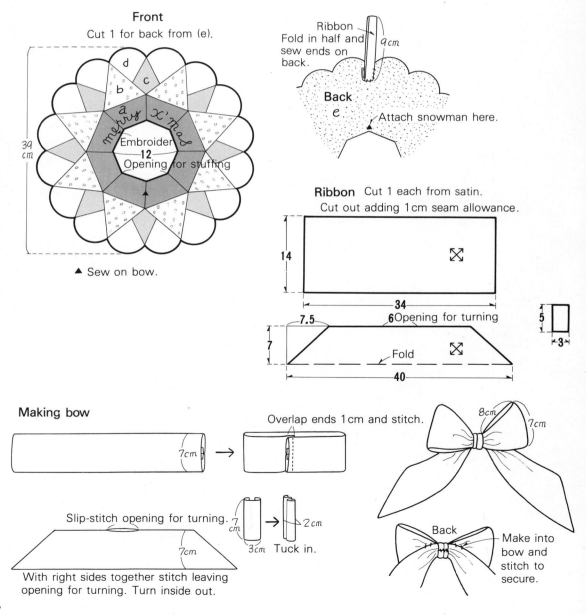

Front
Cut 1 for back from (e).

d
b c
a
merry X'mas
Embroider
12
Opening for stuffing

39 cm

▲ Sew on bow.

Ribbon
Fold in half and sew ends on back.
9 cm

Back
e
Attach snowman here. ▲

Ribbon Cut 1 each from satin.
Cut out adding 1 cm seam allowance.

14
34
6 Opening for turning
7.5
7
Fold
40
5
3

Making bow

7 cm → Overlap ends 1 cm and stitch.

8 cm 7 cm

Slip-stitch opening for turning.
7 cm
7 cm
7 cm → 2 cm
3 cm Tuck in.

With right sides together stitch leaving opening for turning. Turn inside out.

Back
Make into bow and stitch to secure.

34

Patterns (Actual size)

Add 0.7 cm seam allowance.

$\frac{1}{8}$

d
Cut 16

c
Cut 8

Embroidery Pattern
Chain-stitch with 3 strands
of floss in white.

b
Cut 8

a
Cut 8

Snowman

Opening for stuffing

No seam allowance on felt.

Head
Cut 2 in white.

Cap
Cut 2 in black.

Arm
Cut 2 in white.

Opening for stuffing

Body
Cut 2 in white.

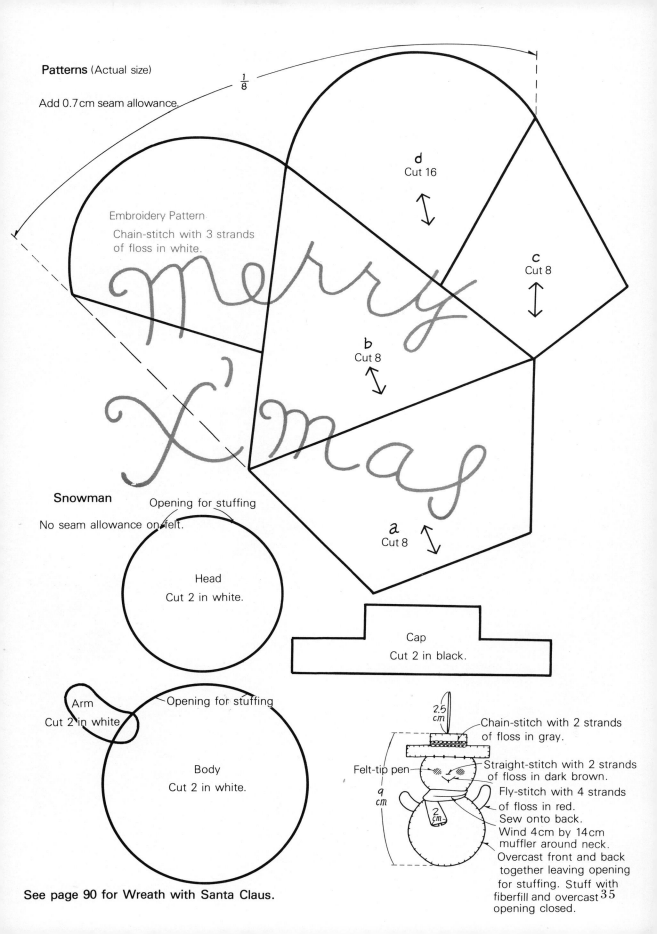

2.5 cm

Chain-stitch with 2 strands
of floss in gray.

Felt-tip pen

Straight-stitch with 2 strands
of floss in dark brown.

9 cm

Fly-stitch with 4 strands
of floss in red.
Sew onto back.
Wind 4 cm by 14 cm
muffler around neck.
Overcast front and back
together leaving opening
for stuffing. Stuff with
fiberfill and overcast
opening closed.

2 cm

See page 90 for Wreath with Santa Claus.

35

Lovely Patchwork

NORTH CAROLINA LILY WALL HANGING
Instructions on page 39.

Framed Patchwork, *shown on page 36.*

MATERIALS

FABRIC: Cotton fabric: Small amount each for patches and appliques (see photo). Polyester fiberfill. White frame, 12.5 cm (inside measurements). Cardboard, 13.2 cm square. Star-shaped green spangles (medium) and transparent beads, 4 each for Yellow Heart. Star-shaped spangles (small), 5 blue & 4 silver; 9 transparent beads for Blue-Gray Heart. Star-shaped red spangles (medium) and transparent beads, 4 each for Red Heart.
FINISHED SIZE: Same size as frame.

DIRECTIONS:

1. Cut out patches and sew them together by hand.
2. Appliqué hearts, padding with fiberfill. Sew on spangles with beads.
3. Place fiberfill thinly over cardboard. Place pieced top over fiberfill and turn back seam allowance. Fix fabric with Scotch tape.
4. Frame.

Add 0.7 cm seam allowance for piecing.
Add 2 cm seam allowances to edges to be framed.

Appliqué patterns (Actual size)

Add 0.7 cm seam allowance.
Pad with fiberfill and appliqué in slip stitch.

Yellow Heart ....Yellow
Blue-Gray Heart ... Blue-Gray
Red Heart ... Red
Cut 4 each

Yellow heart

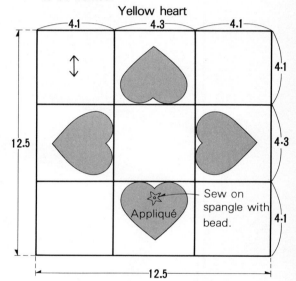

Sew on spangle with bead.
Appliqué

Red heart

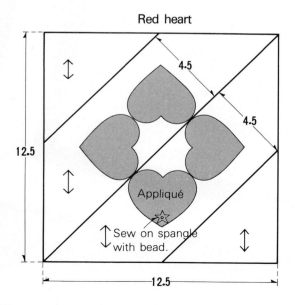

Appliqué
Sew on spangle with bead.

Bule-gray heart

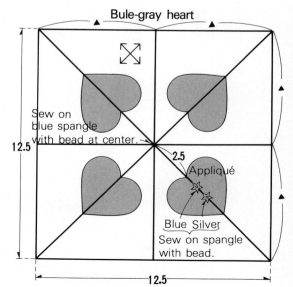

Sew on blue spangle with bead at center.
Appliqué
Blue Silver
Sew on spangle with bead.

North Carolina Lily Wall Hanging,
shown on page 37.

MATERIALS

FABRICS: Sheeting: (a) white, 90cm by 130cm; (c) green, 35 cm by 15 cm; (f) navy, 90cm by 30cm. Floral prints: (b) 30cm by 15cm; (d, e) 15 cm by 20cm each. Thin quilt batting, 70cm square. Quilting thread in white, navy and green.

FINISHED SIZE: 70cm square.

DIRECTIONS:

1. Cut out patches. Appliqué stems and handles in place. Then sew patches together by hand.
2. Transfer quilting patterns onto pieced top. Pin and baste top, batting and lining together.
3. Quilt along seams of patches with matching quilting thread. Then quilt birds and border patterns.
4. Bind edges to finish.

Piecing

Sew patches in numerical order.

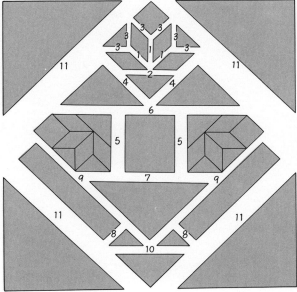

Cutting

Top piece
  Add 0.7cm seam allowance.

	7cm × 68cm	Cut 2
	7cm × 54cm	Cut 2
	24cm triangle	Cut 4
a	12cm ⁄	Cut 2
	10cm ⁄	Cut 1
	24cm × 5cm	Cut 2
	12cm × 10cm	Cut 1
b	17cm triangle	Cut 1
	5cm ⁄	Cut 2
f	3cm × 48cm	Cut 2
	3cm × 54cm	Cut 2

See patterns for flowers.
Cut batting 70cm square.
Lining Cut 1 70cm square
for lining from (a).

Strip for binding

See page 18 for mitered corner.

Actual-size patterns are on page 93.

CRIB QUILTS

Duck Quilt Instructions on page 101.
Baby Quilt Instructions on page 42.

MATERIALS

FABRICS: Yellow and white gingham checks, 73 cm by 243 cm. Cotton broadcloth: Unbleached and white, 71 cm square each; yellow, 60 cm by 30 cm; small amount for appliques. Thick quilt batting, 120 cm by 90 cm. Quilt batting, 120 cm by 30 cm. White quilting thread. White cotton lace edging: 3.5 cm by 40 cm; 2.5 cm by 80 cm. One pink button, 1.7 cm in diameter. Six-strand embroidery floss, No. 25: Pink, light pink, yellow green, dark yellow green, light olive green, blue, light blue, gray and peony rose.

FINISHED SIZE: 118.5 cm by 86 cm.

DIRECTIONS:

1. Cut out patches and sew 6 squares together by machine.
2. Place smaller patches (a-c) and batting on pieced top and sew on in slip stitch.
3. Sew border strips around top piece.
4. With right sides facing, sew lining and top together, leaving opening for turning. Turn inside out. Insert batting and slip-stitch opening closed.
5. Quilt along seams. Appliqué from 1 to 6.

Cutting

Top piece … Add 1.5 cm seam allowance.
Cut 3 pieces each of 32.5 cm square from unbleached and white cotton broadcloth. Cut 4 pieces from gingham checks for border. See patterns for a-c.

Batting
Cut 118.5 cm by 86 cm from thick quilt batting.

Lining
Cut 2 pieces of 121.5 cm by 46 cm from gingham checks and sew them together with 1.5 cm seams to make 121.5 cm by 89 cm. Sew 40 cm from each side leaving center open for turning.

Yellow cotton broadcloth …
  Add 1 cm
    seam allowance.
Batting …
  No seam allowance.

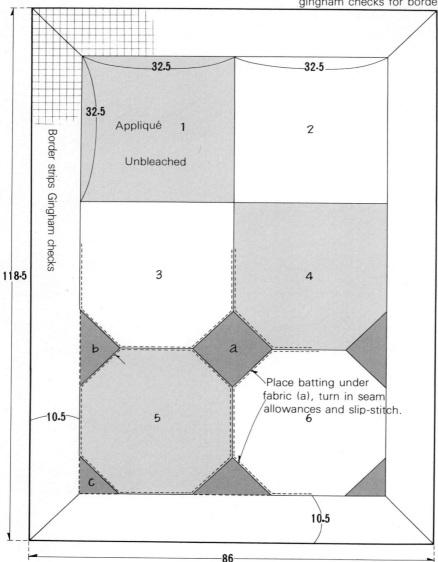

Appliqué patterns Add 0.8cm seam allowance for fabric. No seam allowance for batting.
Place appliqués at center of each square and sew in slip stitch catching lining.

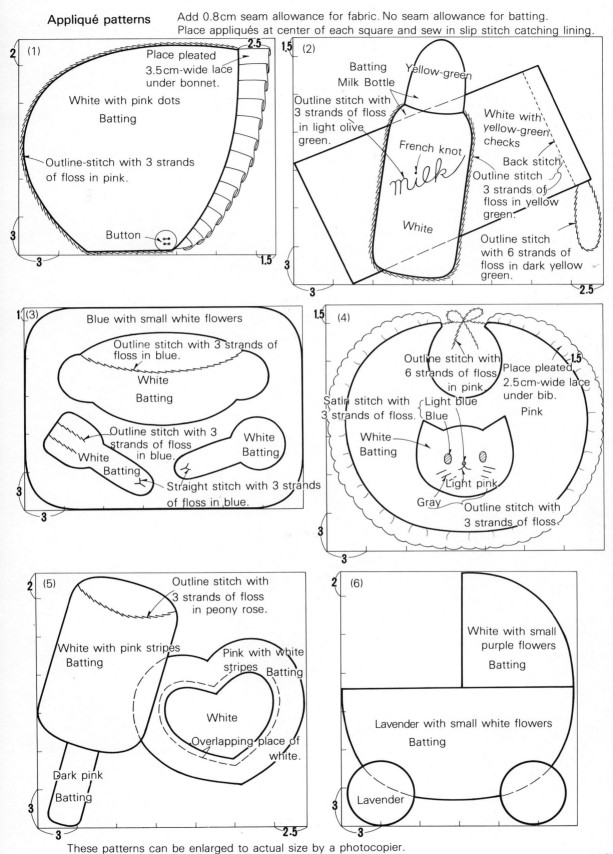

(1)

2

2.5

Place pleated 3.5cm-wide lace under bonnet.

White with pink dots
Batting

Outline-stitch with 3 strands of floss in pink.

3

Button

3   3   1.5

(2)

1.5

Batting
Milk Bottle   Yellow-green

Outline stitch with 3 strands of floss in light olive green.

French knot
milk

White

White with yellow-green checks

Back stitch

Outline stitch 3 strands of floss in yellow green.

Outline stitch with 6 strands of floss in dark yellow green.

3   3   2.5

(3)

1

Blue with small white flowers

Outline stitch with 3 strands of floss in blue.

White
Batting

Outline stitch with 3 strands of floss in blue.

White
Batting

White
Batting

Straight stitch with 3 strands of floss in blue.

3   3

(4)

1.5

Outline stitch with 6 strands of floss in pink.

Place pleated 2.5cm-wide lace under bib.

1.5

Satin stitch with 3 strands of floss.

Light blue
Blue

Pink

White
Batting

Light pink

Gray

Outline stitch with 3 strands of floss.

3

(5)

2

Outline stitch with 3 strands of floss in peony rose.

White with pink stripes
Batting

Pink with white stripes
Batting

White

Overlapping place of white.

Dark pink
Batting

3
3   2.5

(6)

2

White with small purple flowers
Batting

Lavender with small white flowers
Batting

Lavender

3   3

These patterns can be enlarged to actual size by a photocopier.

43

POCHETTES, PURSES AND TOTE BAGS
Instructions for Pochettes on page 46,
for Purses on page 97 and for Tote Bags on page 98.

CORNUCOPIA
MATERIALS

FABRICS: Cotton fabric: Red, 90cm square; white, 50cm by 25cm; sage green, small amount; 6 different prints in tints of red, small amount each; for backing, 42cm by 22cm; for lining, 32cm by 42cm. Quilt batting, 42cm by 22cm. Outing flannel, 120cm by 5cm. White quilting thread. 20cm zipper. Red leather string, 20cm.

FINISHED SIZE: See diagram.

DIRECTIONS:

1. Cut out patches adding 0.7 cm seam allowance. Add 1cm seam allowance to two sides of triangle. Sew patches together by hand.
2. Sew bottoms of front and back together. Draw quilting lines. Pin and baste top, batting and backing together. Quilt.
3. Make shoulder strap and strap holders.

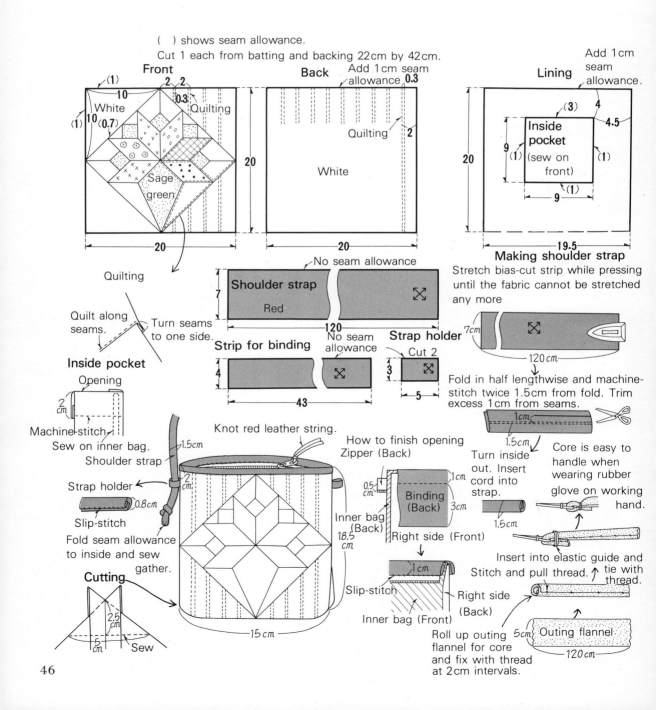

( ) shows seam allowance.
Cut 1 each from batting and backing 22cm by 42cm.

4. With right sides facing and strap holders in between, sew side seams of front and back catching holders. Sew corners of bottom for gusset.
5. Sew inside pocket onto lining. Sew side seams and corners of bottom.
6. Insert lining into bag with wrong sides together. Sew on zipper.
7. Insert end of strap into holder and tie end.

Patterns (Actual size)

Add 0.7 cm seam allowance.

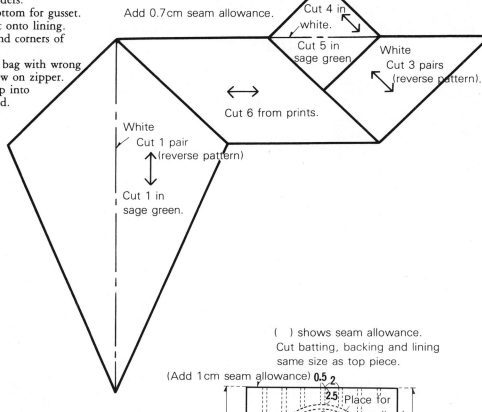

Cut 4 in white.

Cut 5 in sage green

White
Cut 3 pairs
(reverse pattern).

Cut 6 from prints.

White
Cut 1 pair
(reverse pattern)

Cut 1 in sage green.

( ) shows seam allowance.
Cut batting, backing and lining same size as top piece.

(Add 1 cm seam allowance)

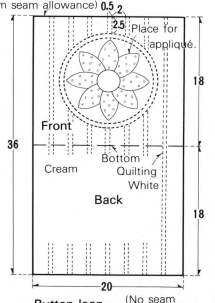

Place for appliqué.

Front

Cream

Bottom
Quilting
White

Back

Button loop

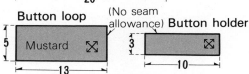

Mustard

(No seam allowance) **Button holder**

Cut shoulder strap, strip for binding and strap holder in same manner as CORNUCOPIA.
See opposite page for inside pocket.

FLOWER
MATERIALS
FABRICS: Cotton fabric: Mustard, 90 cm square; cream, 38 cm by 22 cm; 9 different floral prints, small amount each; for backing, 38 cm by 22 cm; for lining, 33 cm by 38 cm. Quilt batting, 38 cm by 22 cm. Outing flannel, 120 cm by 6 cm. White and navy quilting thread. One 5 cm bamboo button.
FINISHED SIZE: See diagram.
DIRECTIONS:
1. Draw quilting lines and mark place for appliques. Cut out appliques and appliqué in place.
2. Pin and baste appliquéd piece, batting and backing together. Quilt.
3. Make shoulder strap and strap holders in same manner as CORNUCOPIA. Make button loop and button holder.
4. Fold in half with right sides together, sew side seams catching strap holders. Sew corners of bottom.
5. Sew lining as for CORNUCOPIA. Sew on inside pocket. Sew side seams and corners of bottom.
6. Bind edges for opening as shown on page 96.
7. Insert end of strap into holder and tie end.

(Continue to page 96)

47

Brighten Up the Kitchen

A: PLACEMAT   B: NAPKIN   C: CENTERPIECE   D: TEA COZY   E: MAT

48

Instructions for A & B on page 50, for C on page 51 and for D & E on page 99.

49

A: Placemat, shown on pages 48 & 49.

MATERIALS (FOR ONE)
FABRIC: Cotton fabric: (a) stripes, 26cm square; (b) dots, 35cm by 25cm; (c) floral prints, 15cm by 10cm; (d) large checks, 23cm by 12cm; (e) small checks, 50.5cm by 37cm.
FINISHED SIZE: 44.5cm by 31cm.

DIRECTIONS:
Cut out patches adding 0.7cm seam allowance. Sew them together by hand. Place top on lining with wrong sides together. Turn lining over top, turn in seam allowance and slip-stitch.

How to finish seam allowance
Turn in seam allowance and slip-stitch.

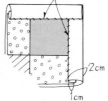

2cm

1cm

Turn lining over top.

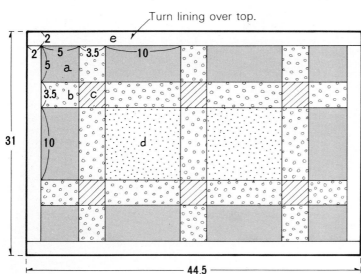

2
2
5
5
a
3.5
3.5
b
c
e
10
10
d
31
44.5

Cutting (For one)
Top piece Add 0.7cm seam allowance

a	5cm square	Cut 4
	5cm × 10cm	Cut 6
b	3.5cm × 10cm	Cut 7
	3.5cm × 5cm	Cut 10
c	3.5cm square	Cut 6
d	10cm square	Cut 2

Lining Cut out 50.5cm by 37cm from (e)

B: Napkins, shown on pages 48 & 49.

MATERIALS (FOR ONE)
FABRIC: Cotton fabric: (e) small checks, 54cm by 50cm; (a) stripes, (b) dots, (c) floral prints, small amount each.
FINISHED SIZE: 52cm by 48cm.
DIRECTIONS:
Cut fabric adding seam allowance. Appliqué in place. Fold edges twice and machine-stitch.

Add 1cm seam allowance.

Finishing

Fold twice and machine stitch.

0.6cm
0.4cm

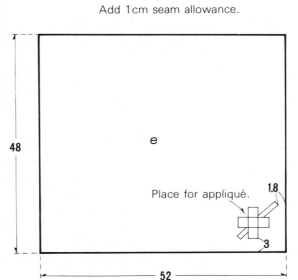

48

e

Place for appliqué.

1.8

3

52

Appliqué patterns
(Actual size)

Add 0.3cm seam allowance for a, and 0.7cm seam allowance for b, c.

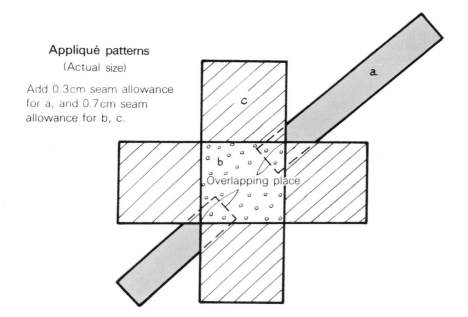

c

a

b

Overlapping place

  C: Centerpiece, shown on pages 48 & 49.

MATERIALS
FABRIC: Cotton fabric. (a-i) small amount each of 9 different prints for patches; for lining, small checks, 38 cm by 25 cm.
FINISHED SIZE: 34 cm by 21 cm.

DIRECTIONS:
Cut out patches and sew them together by hand. Place pieced top on lining with wrong sides together. Turn lining over top, turn in seam allowance and slip-stitch.

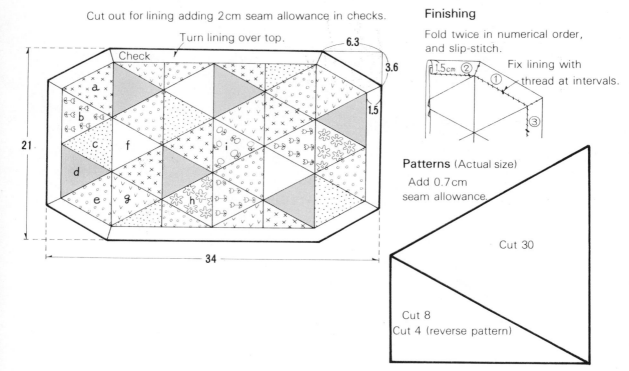

Cut out for lining adding 2cm seam allowance in checks.

Turn lining over top.

Check

6.3

3.6

1.5

21

34

a b c d e f g h i

Finishing
Fold twice in numerical order, and slip-stitch.

1.5cm ② ① Fix lining with thread at intervals. ③

Patterns (Actual size)
Add 0.7cm seam allowance.

Cut 30

Cut 8
Cut 4 (reverse pattern)

51

KITCHEN ACCESSORIES

Toaster Oven Cover Instructions on page 119.
Electric Cooker Cover Instructions on page 117.
Pot Holders Instructions on page 54.

ANVIL, shown at left
MATERIALS
FABRICS: Cotton fabric: Beige, 35cm by 20cm; dark brown with white dots, 18cm by 28cm; brown and white stripes, 17cm square; small amount of brick red; lining, 17cm square. Outing flannel, 34cm by 17cm. White quilting thread.
FINISHED SIZE: 17cm square.

DIRECTIONS:
1. Cut out patches and sew them together by hand.
2. Pin and baste pieced top, outing flannel and lining together. Quilt along 0.5cm inside of each patch.
3. Pin and baste back piece, outing flannel and lining together. Quilt diagonally in two directions at 2.5cm intervals.
4. Pin and baste front and back together with wrong sides facing. Bind edges to finish, catching ends of hanging loop in place.

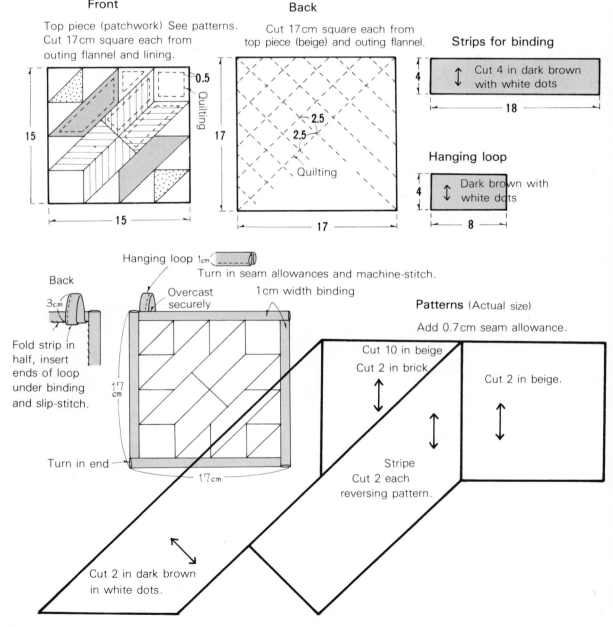

Front

Top piece (patchwork) See patterns.
Cut 17cm square each from
outing flannel and lining.

0.5
Quilting
15
15

Back

Cut 17cm square each from
top piece (beige) and outing flannel.

17
17
2.5
2.5
Quilting

Strips for binding

Cut 4 in dark brown
with white dots
4
18

Hanging loop

Dark brown with
white dots
4
8

Back

3cm
Fold strip in half, insert ends of loop under binding and slip-stitch.
Turn in end

Hanging loop 1cm
Turn in seam allowances and machine-stitch.
Overcast securely
1cm width binding
17cm
17cm

Patterns (Actual size)

Add 0.7cm seam allowance.

Cut 10 in beige
Cut 2 in brick

Cut 2 in beige.

Stripe
Cut 2 each
reversing pattern.

Cut 2 in dark brown
in white dots.

54

DUTCH MILL, shown at right
MATERIALS
FABRICS: Cotton fabric: Red with small flowers, 25 cm
by 20 cm; green, 18 cm by 21 cm; unbleached, 25 cm by
15 cm; small amount each of floral prints with white,
yellow and blue background; for lining, 17 cm square.
Outing flannel, 34 cm by 17 cm. White quilting thread.

FINISHED SIZE: 17 cm square.
DIRECTIONS: Make in same manner as ANVIL.

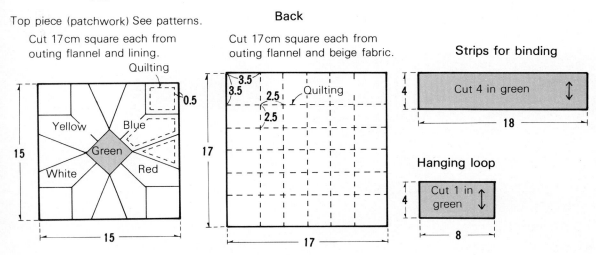

Front

Top piece (patchwork) See patterns.

Cut 17 cm square each from
outing flannel and lining.

Quilting

Yellow   Blue
Green
White   Red

15

15

Back

Cut 17 cm square each from
outing flannel and beige fabric.

3.5
3.5   2.5   Quilting
2.5

17

17

Strips for binding

Cut 4 in green

4

18

Hanging loop

Cut 1 in
green

4

8

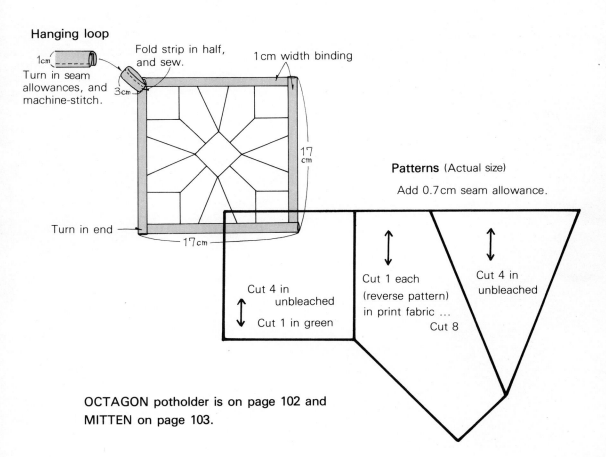

Hanging loop

1 cm

Turn in seam
allowances, and
machine-stitch.

Fold strip in half,
and sew.

3 cm

1 cm width binding

Turn in end

17 cm

17 cm

Patterns (Actual size)

Add 0.7 cm seam allowance.

Cut 4 in
unbleached

Cut 1 in green

Cut 1 each
(reverse pattern)
in print fabric ...

Cut 8

Cut 4 in
unbleached

OCTAGON potholder is on page 102 and
MITTEN on page 103.

COMFORTABLE BEDROOMS

CHURN DASH BEDSPREAD

Instructions on page 58.

Fabrics Used (Actual Size)

Churn Dash Bedspread,
shown on pages 56 & 57.

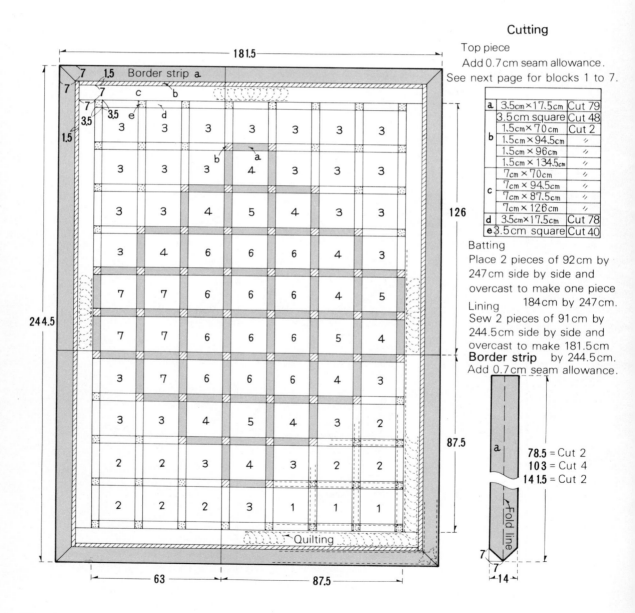

MATERIALS

FABRICS: Cotton fabric: (a) 90cm by 260cm; (b) 90cm by 140cm; (c) 90cm by130cm; (d) 90cm by 95cm; (e) 90cm by 65cm; (f, g) 90cm by 30cm each; (h) 50cm by 20cm; (i) 90cm square; (j) 90cm by 10cm; (k) 90cm by 80cm; (l) 90cm by 60cm; (m) 90cm by 30cm; (n, o) 90cm by 20cm each; (p) 90cm by 40cm; (q) 20cm by 15cm. Sheeting for lining, 91cm by 490cm. Quilt batting, 92cm by 5m. White quilting thread.
FINISHED SIZE: 244.5cm by 181.5cm.

DIRECTIONS:

1. Cut out patches and sew them together by hand. Make required pieces of 7 different blocks. Join 10 by blocks.
2. Sew border (b) & (c) to pieced blocks. Transfer quilting patterns to (c).
3. Sew pieces of batting and lining together.
4. Pin and baste pieced top, batting and lining together. Quilt along inside of center patches and diagonal lines of each block starting from center.
5. Bind edges with (a) and quilt at corners, along seams and folded edges.

Cutting

Top piece
Add 0.7cm seam allowance.
See next page for blocks 1 to 7.

a	3.5cm×17.5cm	Cut 79
	3.5cm square	Cut 48
b	1.5cm×70cm	Cut 2
	1.5cm×94.5cm	〃
	1.5cm×96cm	〃
	1.5cm×134.5cm	〃
c	7cm×70cm	〃
	7cm×94.5cm	〃
	7cm×87.5cm	〃
	7cm×126cm	〃
d	3.5cm×17.5cm	Cut 78
e	3.5cm square	Cut 40

Batting
Place 2 pieces of 92cm by 247cm side by side and overcast to make one piece 184cm by 247cm.

Lining
Sew 2 pieces of 91cm by 244.5cm side by side and overcast to make 181.5cm by 244.5cm.

Border strip
Add 0.7cm seam allowance.

78.5 = Cut 2
103 = Cut 4
141.5 = Cut 2

Motif

Add 0.7 cm seam allowance.

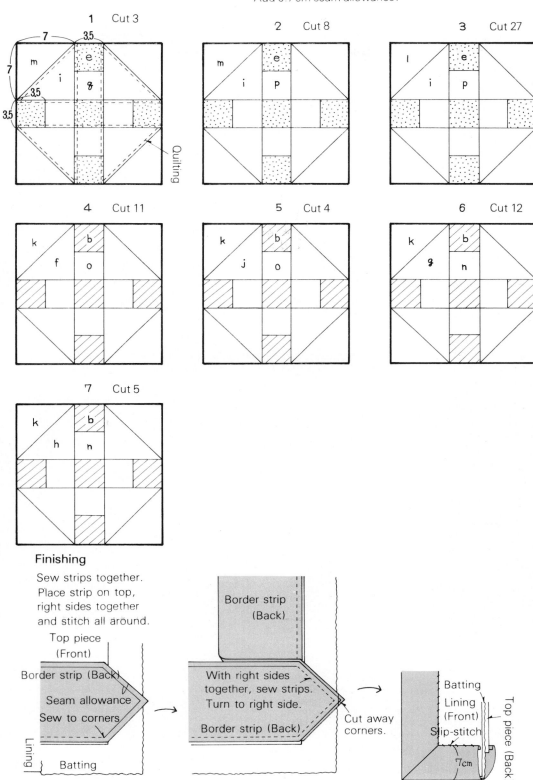

Finishing

Sew strips together.
Place strip on top,
right sides together
and stitch all around.

Top piece (Front)

Border strip (Back)

Seam allowance

Sew to corners.

Lining

Batting

Border strip (Back)

With right sides
together, sew strips.
Turn to right side.

Border strip (Back)

Cut away corners.

Batting

Lining (Front)

Slip-stitch

Top piece (Back)

7cm

Quilting patterns are on page 106.

*Fabrics Used
(Actual Size)
For Muffler*

a

b

c

d

QUILTED HAPPI COATS FOR MOTHER AND CHILD

Instructions for Happi Coat for Mother on page 62,
for Child on page 106 and for Muffler on page 105.

*Fabrics Used (Actual Size)
For Mother*

a

b

c

d

e

Fabrics Used (Actual Size) For Child

61

MATERIALS

FABRICS: Cotton fabric: (e) navy, 90 cm by 320 cm; (a-d) 30 cm by 15 cm each. Fabrics for backing and lining, 90 cm by 280 cm each. Quilt batting, 70 cm by 280 cm. Thin quilt batting for pocket, 42 cm by 21 cm. White quilting thread.

FINISHED SIZE: Width across back, 64 cm. Length, 69.5 cm. Sleeve length from center back, 63 cm.
DIRECTIONS:
1. Cut out left and right pieces following diagram.
2. Cut out patches and sew them together by hand.

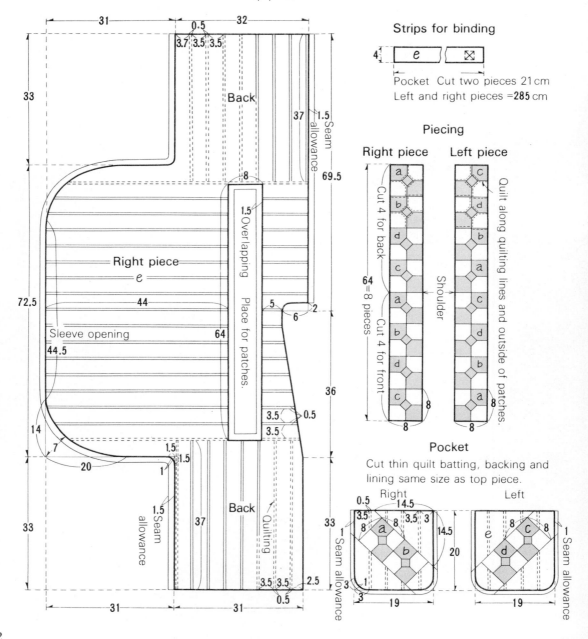

Cut out left piece (reverse pattern).
Cut batting, backing and lining same size as top piece.

Strips for binding

Pocket Cut two pieces 21 cm
Left and right pieces = **285 cm**

Piecing

Pocket
Cut thin quilt batting, backing and lining same size as top piece.

3. Sew patches onto left and right pieces in slip stitch.
4. Sew back seams of top, backing and lining individually and press seams open. Overlap 3 cm at center back of batting and sew with large stitches.
5. Mark quilting lines on top.
6. Pin and baste top, batting and backing together. Quilt along quilting lines and outside of patches.
7. Sew patches to pocket pieces. Mark quilting lines.
8. Pin and baste top, batting and backing together and quilt in same way as body.
9. Place lining of pocket on quilted piece. Bind top edges, sew onto body in blind stitch and top-stitch.
10. Sew side and sleeve seams. Press seams open. Make lining in same manner. Insert lining into top and sew sleeve seams of backing and lining together by hand.
11. Turn in seam allowances of sleeve lining 0.5 cm in from sleeve opening and slip-stitch. Fix lining with back stitch.
12. Bind front and bottom edges to finish.

Patterns (Actual size)
Add 0.7 cm seam allowance.

a ~ d   Cut 10 each
e   Cut 40

a ~ d
Cut 5 each

Piecing

Stitch between marks
(don't stitch across seam allowances.)

(1) Sew 3 printed patches (shaded area)
    together and press seams
    toward center.
(2) Sew on solids and press seams
    to print side.
(3) Sew blocks together.
    Press seams to print side.

→ shows direction for turning seams.

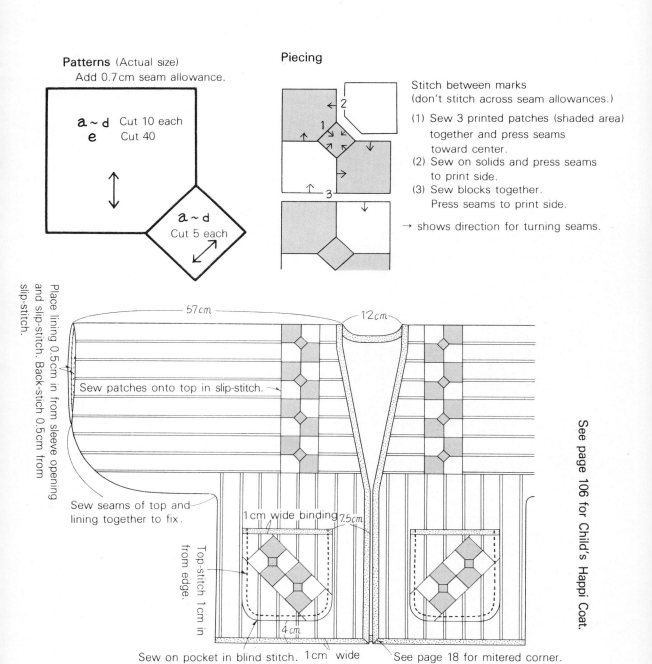

57cm   12cm

Sew patches onto top in slip-stitch.

Sew seams of top and lining together to fix.

Place lining 0.5cm in from sleeve opening and slip-stitch. Back-stitch 0.5cm from slip-stitch.

Top-stitch 1cm in from edge.

1cm wide binding   7.5cm

4cm

Sew on pocket in blind stitch.   1cm wide binding

See page 18 for mitered corner.

See page 106 for Child's Happi Coat.

HOUSE AND TREE BEDSPREAD

Instructions on page 66.

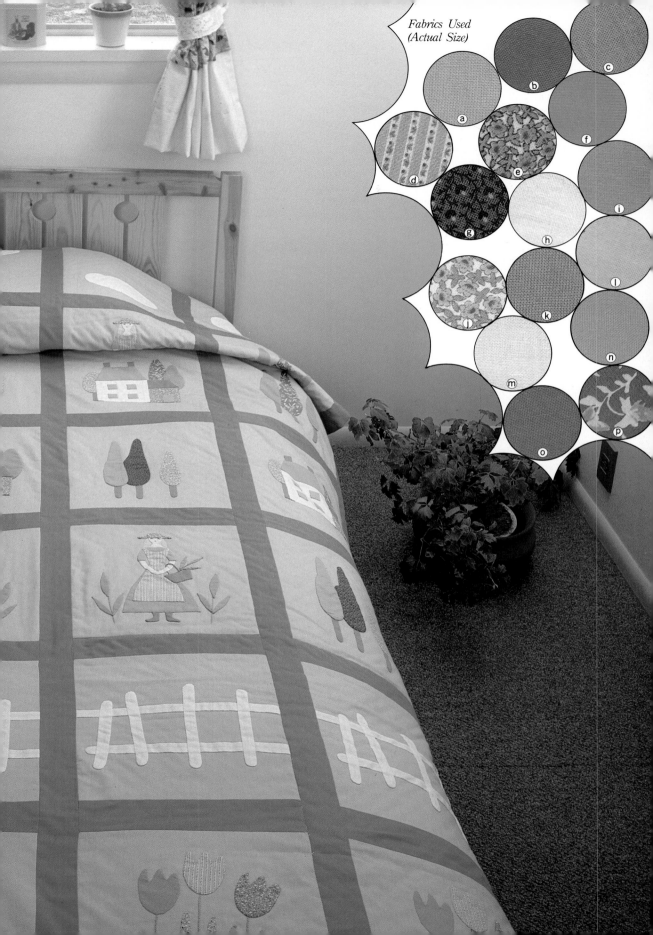

Fabrics Used
(Actual Size)

House and Tree Bedspread, shown on pages 64 & 65.

MATERIALS

FABRICS: Coton fabric: (a) 90 cm by 360 cm; (b) 90 cm by 280 cm; (c) 90 cm by 25 cm; (d) 50 cm by 25 cm; (e) 40 cm by 20 cm; (f) 90 cm by 45 cm; (g) 30 cm by 20 cm; (h) 90 cm by 50 cm; (i) 30 cm by 20 cm; (j) 60 cm by 25 cm; (k) 90 cm by 15 cm; (l,m) small amount each; (n) 40 cm by 20 cm; (o) 35 cm by 15 cm; (p) 50 cm by 20 cm. Quilted fabric for lining, 86 cm by 452 cm. Six-strand embroidery floss, No. 25: Powder green, brown and pink.

FINISHED SIZE: 170 cm by 226 cm.

DIRECTIONS:

1. Cut out required number of squares and border strips. Enlarge appliqué patterns and cut out appliques.
2. Appliqué onto each square following diagram. Place clouds and other appliques from 2 to 7 as indicated matching centers.
3. Machine-stitch 7 squares together in rows with short strips (b) in between, then sew them together with long strips (b) in between.
4. Sew pieces of lining together.
5. Place top on lining with wrong sides facing and sew together with two rows of machine-stitching.
6. Sew border to top.

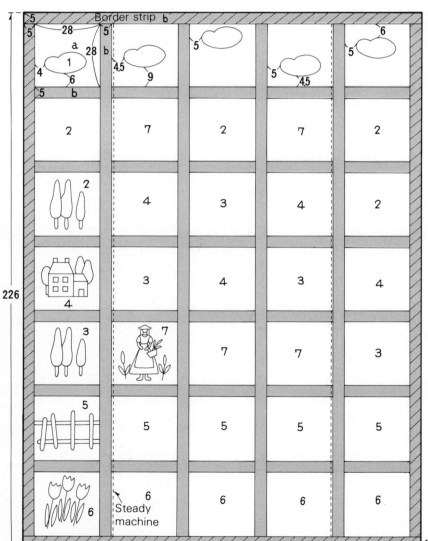

Cutting

Top piece

Add 1 cm seam allowance.

a.....Cut 35 pieces of 28 cm square.

b.....Cut 30 pieces of 5 cm by 28 cm.

Cut 4 pieces of 5 cm by 216 cm.

Lining

Sew 2 pieces of 86 cm by 226 cm together with 1 cm seams to make one piece 170 cm by 226 cm.

See page 2 for finishing corners.

Border strip   Add 1 cm seam allowance.

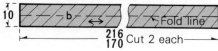

Cut 2 each

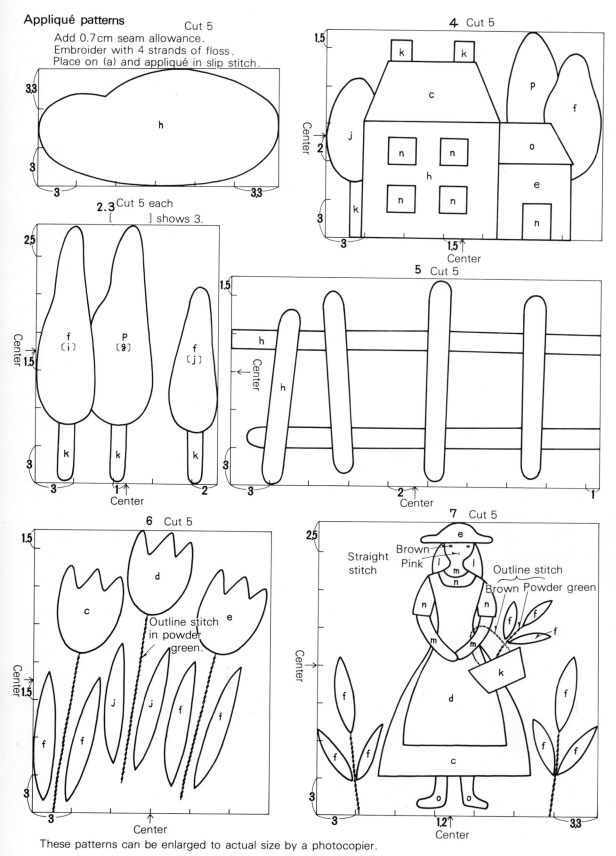

Appliqué patterns

These patterns can be enlarged to actual size by a photocopier.

MODERN PATCHWORK

A: HAIR DRYER CASE   B,C: COSMETIC BAGS
D: PEN CASE   E: GLASSES CASE
F: ALL-PURPOSE BAG

Instructions for A on page 70, for B & C
on page 109, for D & E on page 111
and for F on page 71.

Ⓒ

Ⓓ

Ⓔ

Ⓕ

A: Hair Dryer Case,
shown on pages 68 & 69.

MATERIALS

FABRIC: Cotton fabric: (a) powder green, 60cm by 45cm; (b-e) 4 different prints (see photo) for patches, small amount each; for lining, 60cm by 40cm. Quilt batting, 60cm by 40cm. White quilting thread. Cotton cord, 0.5cm in diameter and 95cm long.

FINISHED SIZE: See diagram.

DIRECTIONS:

1. Cut out patches adding seam allowance. Sew them together by hand. Sew center block and fabric (a).
2. Mark quilting lines on pieced front and back. Pin and baste front and batting together. Quilt. Quilt back in same way.
3. Sew front and back together with right sides facing. Sew corners at bottom. Turn inside out.
4. Make lining in same way.
5. Insert lining into quilted bag with wrong sides together. Turn in seam allowances and slip stitch at each side. Fold top edges and stitch to make casing.
6. Insert cotton cord into casing.

( ) shows seam allowance.
Add 1cm seam allowance unless otherwise indicated.
Cut 2 pieces for quilt batting, 30cm by 40cm each.
Cut 2 pieces for lining, 29.5cm by 40cm each.

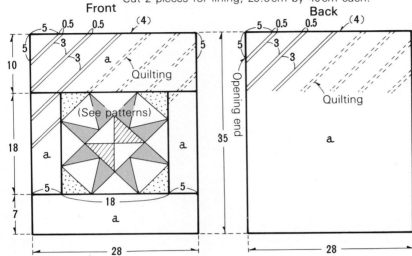

Patterns (Actual size)   Add 0.7cm seam allowance.

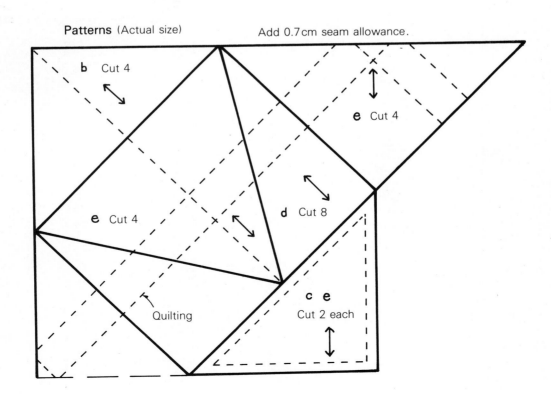

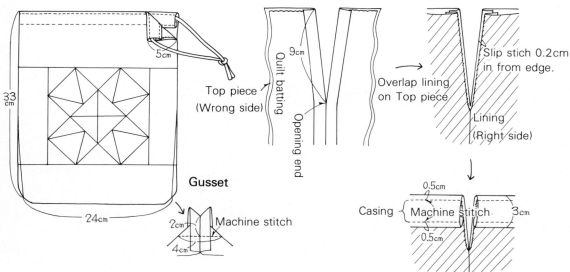

How to make casing

Top piece (Wrong side)

Quilt batting

9cm

Opening end

5cm

33cm

24cm

Gusset

2cm

4cm

Machine stitch

Overlap lining on Top piece

Slip stich 0.2cm in from edge.

Lining (Right side)

0.5cm

Casing Machine stitch 3cm

0.5cm

F: All-purpose Bag, shown on pages 68 & 69.

MATERIALS

FABRIC: Cotton fabric: Off-white, 60cm by 25cm; 9 different prints (see photo) for patches, small amount each; for lining, 50cm by 26cm. Quilt batting, 50cm by 26cm. White quilting thread. One button, 1.8cm in diameter.

FINISHED SIZE: See diagram.

DIRECTIONS:

1. Cut out patches and sew 3 strips together to make square. Make 18 squares and join 3 by 3 squares.

2. Sew bottom seams of front and back together. Mark quilting lines. Pin and baste top and batting together. Quilt.

3. Sew side seams with right sides together. Turn inside out.

4. Make lining in same way. Make button loop.

5. Insert lining into quilted bag with wrong sides together and bind top edges catching ends of button loop.

6. Sew on button.

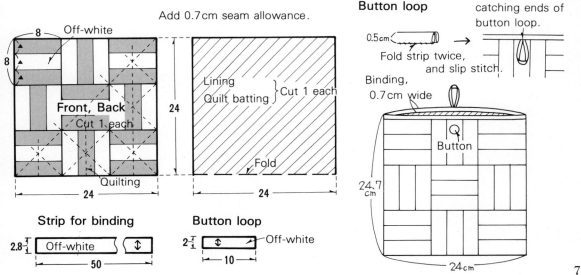

Add 0.7cm seam allowance.

8 Off-white

8

Front, Back
Cut 1 each

Quilting

24

Lining
Quilt batting } Cut 1 each

24

Fold

24

Button loop

Bind top edges catching ends of button loop.

0.5cm

Fold strip twice, and slip stitch.

Binding, 0.7cm wide

Button

24.7cm

24cm

Strip for binding

2.8 Off-white

50

Button loop

2 Off-white

10

A: SEWING BOX   B,C,D,E,F: PINCUSHIONS
G: SCISSORS CASE   H: TELEPHONE   COVER

Instructions for A on page 120, for B—E on page 74, for F on page 121, for G on page 113 and for H on page 123.

FOR B
MATERIALS
FABRIC: Cotton broadcloth: small amount each of pink and soft pink floral prints. Quilt batting, 6 cm square. Pink embroidery floss, No. 25. White cotton lace edging, 1 cm by 35 cm. Cotton for stuffing.

FINISHED SIZE: 10 cm in diameter.

DIRECTIONS:
1. Cut out patches adding seam allowance. Sew prints and solids together alternately by hand.
2. Pin and baste soft pink fabric and batting together. Quilt. Place quilted piece on center of patches and slip-stitch.
3. Cut out back piece. With right sides facing, sew front and back together leaving opening for stuffing. Turn inside out. Stuff with cotton and slip-stitch opening closed.

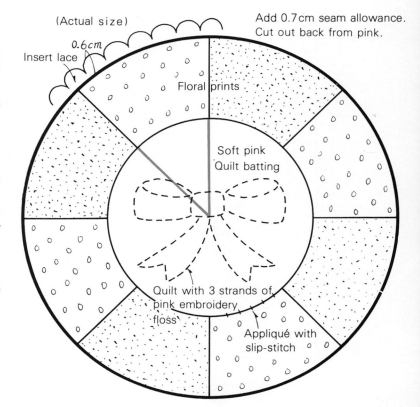

(Actual size)

Add 0.7 cm seam allowance. Cut out back from pink.

0.6 cm
Insert lace

Floral prints

Soft pink
Quilt batting

Quilt with 3 strands of pink embroidery floss

Appliqué with slip-stitch

(Actual size)   Add 0.7 cm seam allowance.
Cut out back piece in blue.

Insert lace between patches and back piece

0.6 cm

Sew ribbon onto patches.

Floral prints

FOR C
MATERIALS
FABRIC: 8 different floral prints; small amount of blue cotton broadcloth. Blue satin ribbon, 0.9 cm by 35 cm. white cotton lace edging, 1 cm by 45 cm. Cotton for stuffing.

FINISHED SIZE: One side of octagon, 4 cm.

DIRECTIONS:
1. Cut out patches adding seam allowance. Sew ribbon onto 4 triangles. Sew triangles together by hand.
2. Make in same way as B.

74

Add 0.7cm seam allowance for sewing together,
and 0.9cm seam allowance for edges.
Cut out back piece in pink.

FOR D
MATERIALS
FABRIC: Cotton broadcloth: Small amount each of pink, orange and 5 different prints. Red bias tape, 1.8cm by 42cm. Cotton for stuffing.

FINISHED SIZE: About 11cm square.

DIRECTIONS:
1. Cut out patches adding seam allowance and sew them together by hand.
2. Cut out back piece. With wrong sides facing, sew front and back together leaving opening for stuffing. Stuff with cotton and slip-stich opening closed.
3. Bind edges with bias tape.

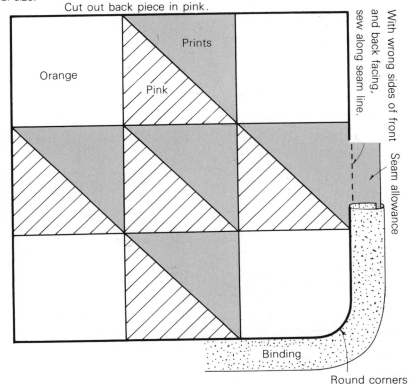

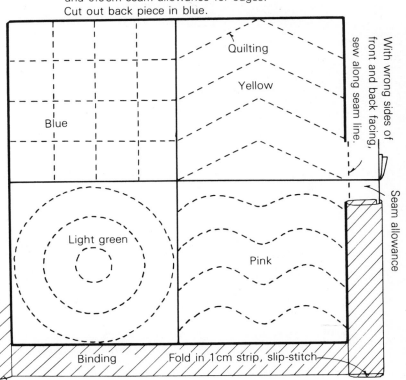

(Actual size)

Add 0.7cm seam allowance for sewing together,
and 0.9cm seam allowance for edges.
Cut out back piece in blue.

FOR E
MATERIALS
FABRIC: Cotton broadcloth: Small amount each of blue, pink, light green and yellow. Quilt batting, 11cm square. Bright yellow bias tape, 1.8cm by 48cm White quilting thread. Cotton for stuffing.

FINISHED SIZE: about 11cm square.

DIRECTIONS:
1. Cut out squares adding seam allowance and sew them together by hand.
2. Pin and baste top and batting together. Quilt.
3. Cut out back piece. Sew quilted front and back together with wrong sides facing leaving opening for stuffing. Stuff with cotton and slip-stitch opening closed.
4. Bind edges with bias tape.

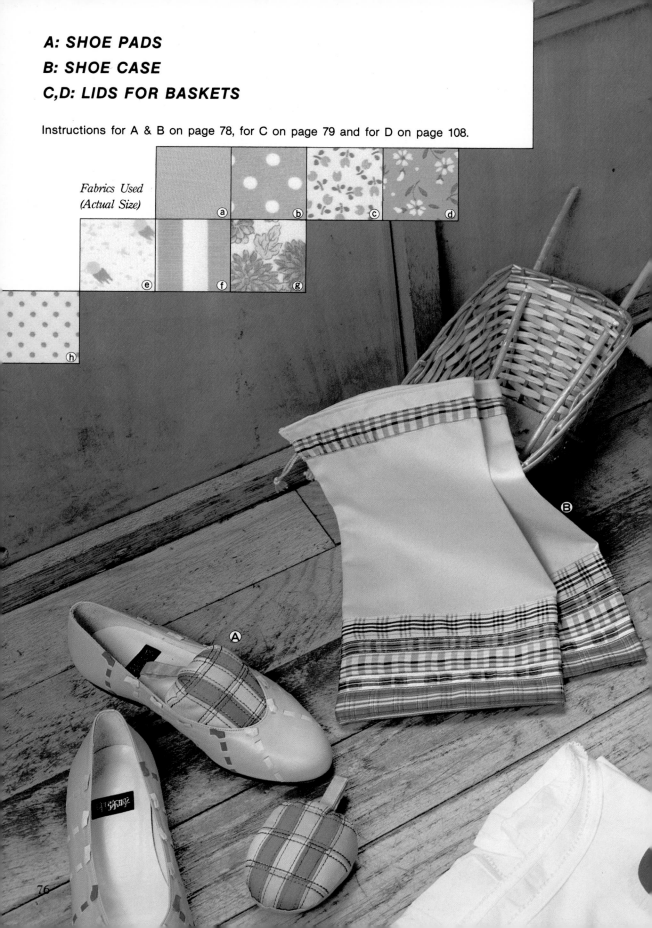

A: SHOE PADS
B: SHOE CASE
C,D: LIDS FOR BASKETS

Instructions for A & B on page 78, for C on page 79 and for D on page 108.

Fabrics Used
(Actual Size)

ⓐ ⓑ ⓒ ⓓ

ⓔ ⓕ ⓖ

ⓗ

Ⓐ Ⓑ

FOR SHOE PADS
MATERIALS (FOR ONE PAIR)
FABRIC: Cotton fabric; salmon pink, 30cm square; small amount each of pink, purple and green. Quilt batting, 25cm by 15cm. Green sewing thread. Polyester fiberfill.

FINISHED SIZE: See diagram.

DIRECTIONS:

1. Cut out patches and sew them together by machine.
2. Machine-stitch pieced front and batting together along seams.
3. Sew front and back together with right sides facing leaving top edge open. Turn inside out.
4. Make loop.
5. Stuff with fiberfill. Turn in seam allowances of top edges, insert ends of loop and sew opening closed. Pull thread and tie knot.

Turn in seam allowances of top edges, insert ends of loop and sew opening closed. Pull thread and tie knot.

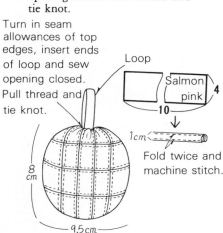

Loop

Salmon pink

4

10

1cm

Fold twice and machine stitch.

8 cm

9.5 cm

Patterns (Actual size)

Add 0.7cm seam allowance.

Cut out 2 pieces each of lining (Salmon pink) and quilt batting same size as top piece.

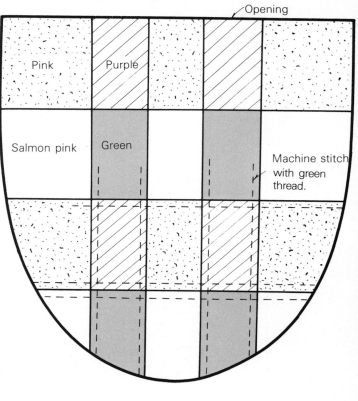

Opening

Pink

Purple

Salmon pink

Green

Machine stitch with green thread.

FOR SHOE CASE
MATERIALS
FABRIC: Pink cotton fabric, 76cm by 34cm. Ribbon: 2.2cm by 152cm; 2 kinds, 1.4cm by 76cm; 2.4cm by 76cm and 2.6cm by 76cm. 2 pieces of pink cotton cord, 0.2cm in diameter and 50cm long each.

FINISHED SIZE: See diagram.

DIRECTIONS:

Sew ribbon onto pink fabric. Fold in half crosswise with right sides together and sew side and bottom seams. Fold seam allowance of opening and stitch. Sew on ribbon for casing. Insert cotton cord into casing.

Add 1cm seam allowance.

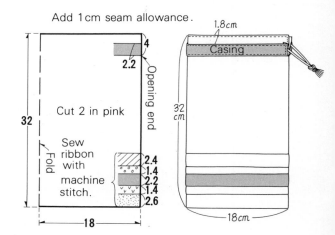

4

2.2

Opening end

32

Cut 2 in pink

Fold

Sew ribbon with machine stitch.

2.4
1.4
2.2
1.4
2.6

18

1.8cm

Casing

32 cm

18cm

Detail of top edge

Fold top edge and stitch.
Then fold side edge and stitch.

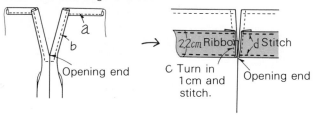

a
b
Opening end

→

22cm Ribbon d Stitch

C Turn in
1cm and
stitch.

Opening end

Coiled Lid for Basket, shown on page 76.

MATERIALS
FABRIC: Cotton fabric: (a) 90cm by 40cm; (b-h) 90cm
by 7cm each. Cotton cord, 0.8cm in diameter and 11cm
long. Cardboard, 30cm in diameter.
FINISHED SIZE: 32cm in diameter.

DIRECTIONS:
Cut out strips and sew them together as indicated. Cover
cotton cord with pieced strip and slip-stitch. Coil and
overcast to fix following diagram. Make ties and sew on
wrong side. Run a gathering stitch around back piece,
cover cardboard and slip-stitch back to wrong side of coil-
ed front.

Making coil

Sew 89 strips together
with 0.5cm seams.
Press seams open.

Place cotton cord
at center.

Cover tightly and
slip-stitch.

Cutting strips and sewing together

Cut out strips 3.5cm wide (8 strips,
60cm long from a. 2 strips each, 90cm long from
b, c, d, e, f, g, h) and sew strips together 12
times in alphbetical order as indicated below.

time

	First	2 ⁒	3·4 ⁒	5·6 ⁒	7·8 ⁒	9·10⁒	11 ⁒	12 ⁒
a	22cm	6cm	8cm	10cm	12cm	14cm	16cm	250cm
b	6 ⁒	6 ⁒	8 ⁒	10 ⁒	12 ⁒	14 ⁒	16 ⁒	
c	6 ⁒	6 ⁒	8 ⁒	10 ⁒	12 ⁒	14 ⁒	16 ⁒	
d	6 ⁒	6 ⁒	8 ⁒	10 ⁒	12 ⁒	14 ⁒	16 ⁒	
e	6 ⁒	6 ⁒	8 ⁒	10 ⁒	12 ⁒	14 ⁒	16 ⁒	
f	6 ⁒	6 ⁒	8 ⁒	10 ⁒	12 ⁒	14 ⁒	16 ⁒	
g	6 ⁒	6 ⁒	8 ⁒	10 ⁒	12 ⁒	14 ⁒	16 ⁒	
h	6 ⁒	6 ⁒	8 ⁒	10 ⁒	12 ⁒	14 ⁒	16 ⁒	

Add 1cm
seam allowance.

Bottom
Cut 1 piece from a.

30

Cord
3¾
Cut 8 pieces from a.
25

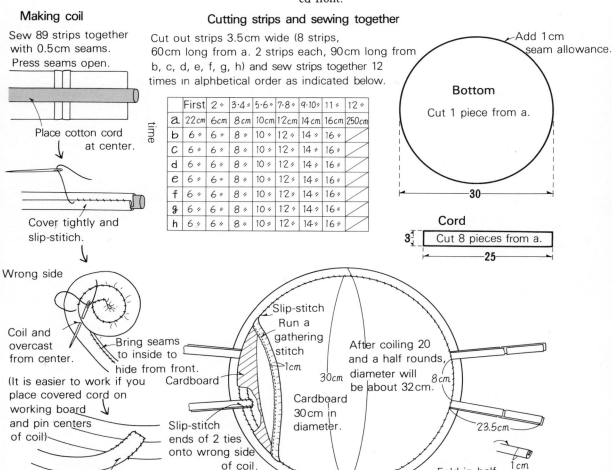

Wrong side

Coil and
overcast
from center.

(It is easier to work if you
place covered cord on
working board
and pin centers
of coil)

Finally, slip-stitch coil
end to wrong side.

Bring seams
to inside to
hide from front.

Cardboard

Slip-stitch
ends of 2 ties
onto wrong side
of coil.

Slip-stitch
Run a
gathering
stitch
1cm

Cardboard
30cm in
diameter.

Turn inside out.
Turn in end and
slip-stitch.

After coiling 20
and a half rounds,
diameter will
be about 32cm.

30cm

8cm

23.5cm

Fold in half
lengthwise
with right
sides together
and stitch.

1cm

79

TISSUE BOX COVER

Instructions on page 81.

COVER WITH YO-YO FLOWERS

MATERIALS

FABRICS: Cotton broadcloth: Cream, 76 cm by 16 cm; salmon pink, 45 cm by 20 cm; powder green, 30 cm square; pink, 20 cm square. Outing flannel, 76 cm by 16 cm. Elastic tape, 2 pieces, 0.8 cm by 14 cm. Soft pink rickrack, 1 cm by 77 cm.

FINISHED SIZE: See diagram.

DIRECTIONS:

1. Cut out patches and machine- stitch together in numerical order.

2. Place pieced patches on outing flannel and machine-stitch along seams.

3. Sew side seams. Fold bottom edges and machine-stitch.

4. Make top following diagram. Sew top and side together with right sides facing and rickrack in between. Turn inside out.

5. Make yo-yo flowers and sew on top.

6. Sew elastic tape onto bottom.

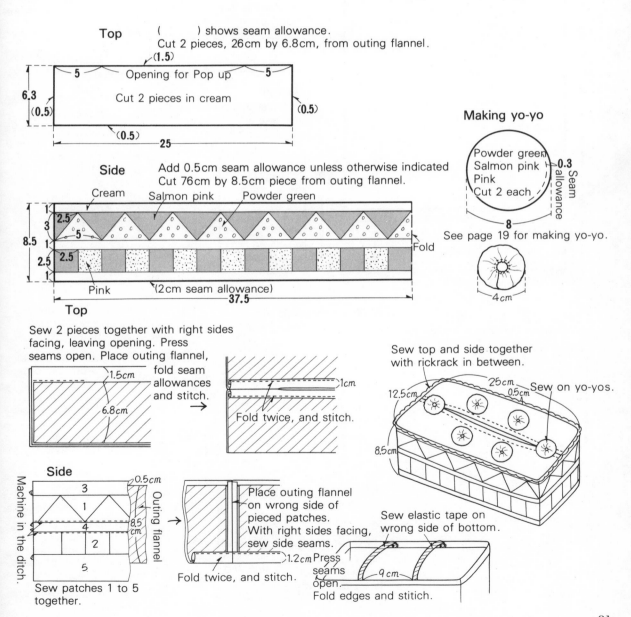

LUNCH BOX TISSUE CASE
MATERIALS
FABRICS: Cotton broadcloth: Red, 90cm by 30cm; dark green, 30cm by 15cm; small amount each of green and cream. Outing flannel, 53cm by 31cm. Red embroidery floss, No. 25. Elastic tape, 2 pieces of 0.8cm by 10cm each. 2 red buttons, 1.5cm in diameter. Polyester fiberfill.

FINISHED SIZE: See diagram.
DIRECTIONS:
Make in numerical order from 1 to 8 following diagram. Stuff top part with fiberfill. (Adjust amount of fiberfill after covering tissue box.)

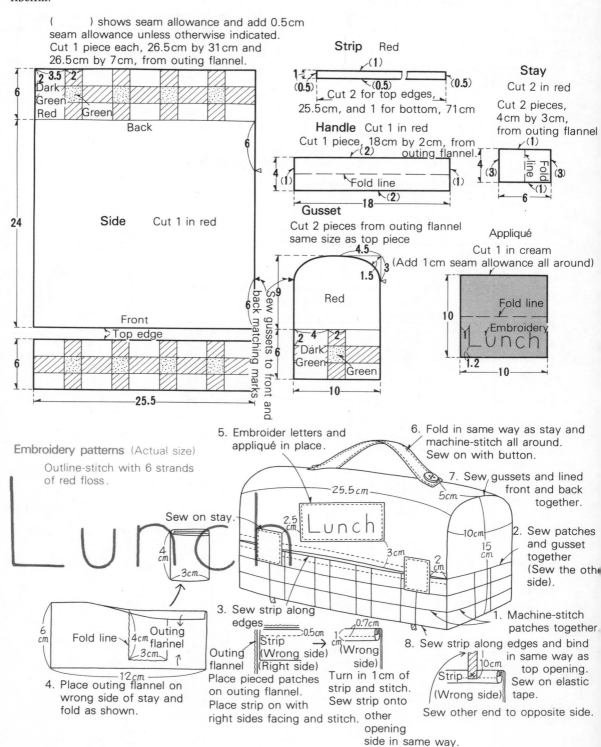

(   ) shows seam allowance and add 0.5cm seam allowance unless otherwise indicated. Cut 1 piece each, 26.5cm by 31cm and 26.5cm by 7cm, from outing flannel.

Strip Red
(1)
1 (0.5) (0.5) (0.5)
Cut 2 for top edges, 25.5cm, and 1 for bottom, 71cm

Stay
Cut 2 in red
Cut 2 pieces, 4cm by 3cm, from outing flannel

Handle Cut 1 in red
Cut 1 piece, 18cm by 2cm, from outing flannel.
(2)
4 (1) Fold line (1)
(2) 18
(1)
4 (3) Fold line (3)
(1)
6

Gusset
Cut 2 pieces from outing flannel same size as top piece
4.5
3
1.5
Red
9
6
Sew gussets to front and back matching marks
6
2 4 2
Dark Green
Green
10

Appliqué
Cut 1 in cream
(Add 1cm seam allowance all around)
Fold line
10
Embroidery
1 Lunch
1.2 10

2 3.5 2
Dark Green
Red Green
6
Back
6
24
Side   Cut 1 in red
Front
Top edge
6
25.5

Embroidery patterns (Actual size)
Outline-stitch with 6 strands of red floss.

Lunch

5. Embroider letters and appliqué in place.

6. Fold in same way as stay and machine-stitch all around. Sew on with button.

7. Sew gussets and lined front and back together.

Sew on stay.
4cm
3cm
25.5cm
2.5cm Lunch
3cm
5cm
10cm
2cm
15cm

2. Sew patches and gusset together (Sew the other side).

1. Machine-stitch patches together.

6cm Fold line 4cm Outing flannel 3cm
12cm

4. Place outing flannel on wrong side of stay and fold as shown.

3. Sew strip along edges
Outing flannel
Strip (Wrong side) (Right side)
0.5cm
Place pieced patches on outing flannel. Place strip on with right sides facing and stitch.

1 cm (Wrong side)
0.7cm
1 cm (Wrong side)
Turn in 1cm of strip and stitch. Sew strip onto other opening side in same way.

8. Sew strip along edges and bind in same way as top opening. Sew on elastic tape.
Strip (Wrong side)
10cm
Sew other end to opposite side.

Continued from page 7

Quilting patterns   (Actual size)

↑
Center

Continued from page 27

Appliqué patterns (Actual size)

Cut out one piece adding 0.5cm seam allowance.
Pad with cotton and appliqué in slip stich.
Work with 3 strands of embroidery thread.

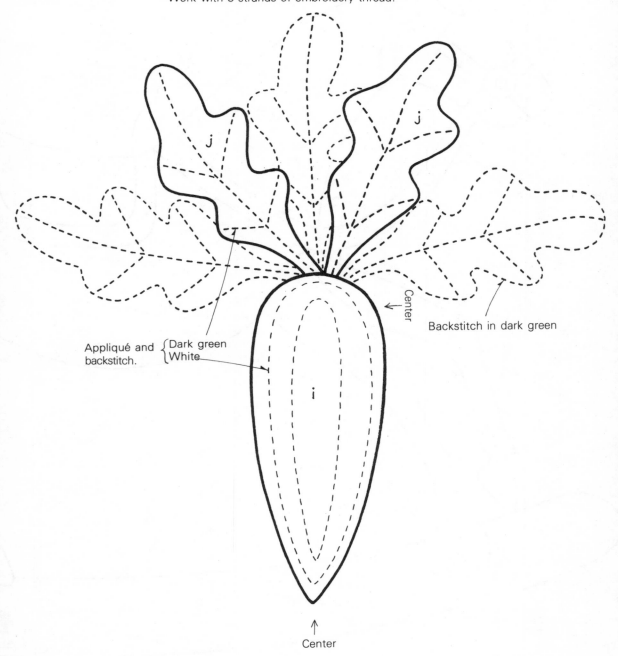

Center

Backstitch in dark green

Appliqué and backstitch. { Dark green White

Center

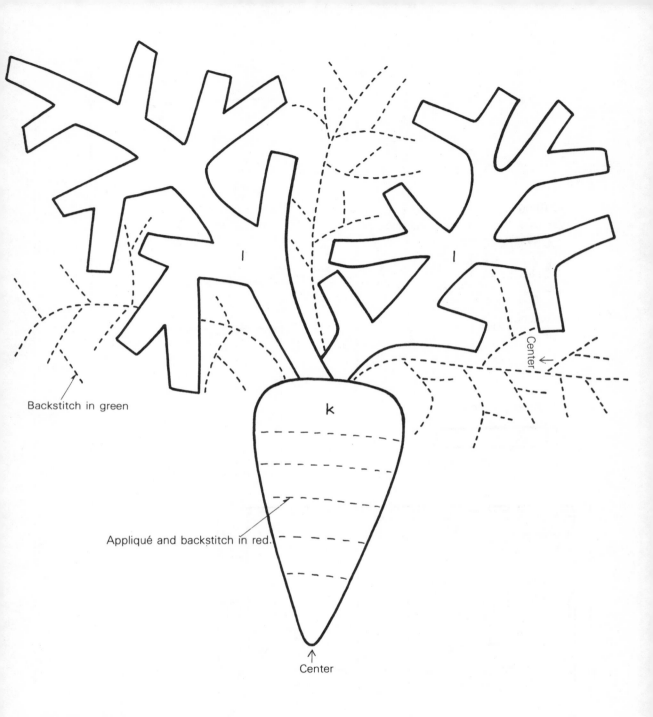

Backstitch in green

Center

k

Appliqué and backstitch in red.

↑
Center

  House Wall Hanging, shown on page 28.

MATERIALS

FABRIC: Cotton fabric: (See photo for colors and designs.) (a) 58 cm square; (b) 90 cm by 28 cm; (c) 7 cm square; (d) 50 cm square; small amount each of 16 different solids and prints for appliques; for lining, 71 cm square. Quilt batting, 71 cm square. White quilting thread. Navy embroidery floss, No. 25.

FINISHED SIZE: 71 cm square.

DIRECTIONS:

1. Cut out patches and borders. Appliqué house onto each square in slip stitch. Embroider date and name.
2. Sew squares together with borders by machine.
3. Pin and baste top, batting and lining together and quilt.
4. Bind edges to finish.

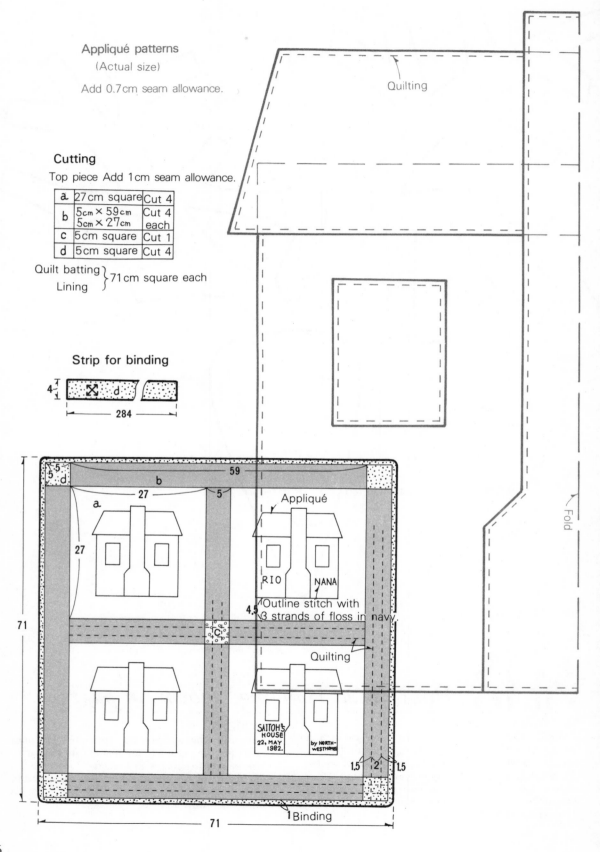

Appliqué patterns

(Actual size)

Add 0.7cm seam allowance.

Quilting

Cutting

Top piece Add 1cm seam allowance.

a	27cm square	Cut 4
b	5cm × 59cm 5cm × 27cm	Cut 4 each
c	5cm square	Cut 1
d	5cm square	Cut 4

Quilt batting
Lining } 71cm square each

Strip for binding

4 ⟮ ⋅⋅⋅ d ⋅⋅⋅ ⟯

284

5.5
5 d
59
b
27
5
a
27
Appliqué
RIO   NANA
4.5
Outline stitch with
3 strands of floss in navy.
C
Quilting
71
SAITOH'S
HOUSE
22, MAY
1982.
by NORTH-
WESTHAME
1.5 2 1.5
Fold
71
Binding

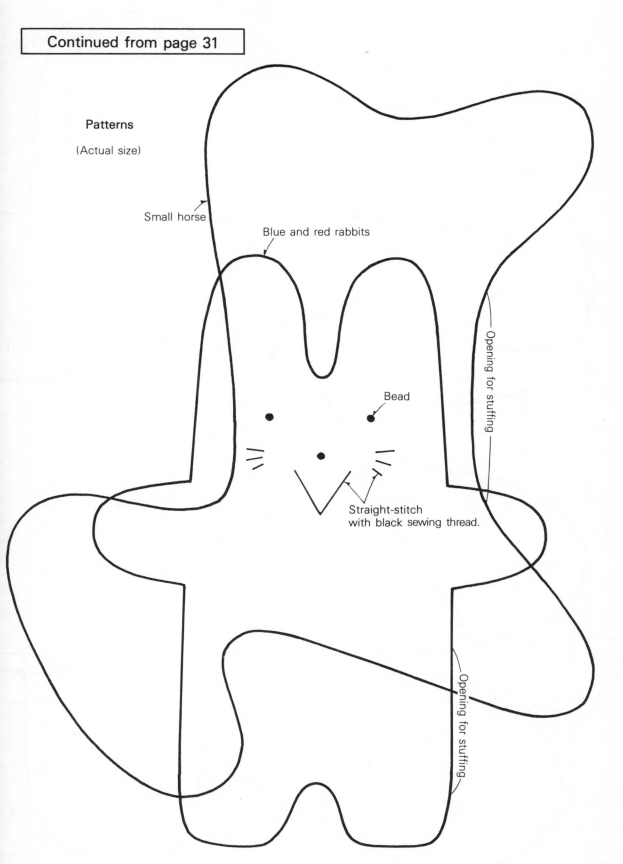

Patterns

(Actual size)

Small horse

Blue and red rabbits

Bead

Opening for stuffing

Straight-stitch
with black sewing thread.

Opening for stuffing

Patterns (Actual size)

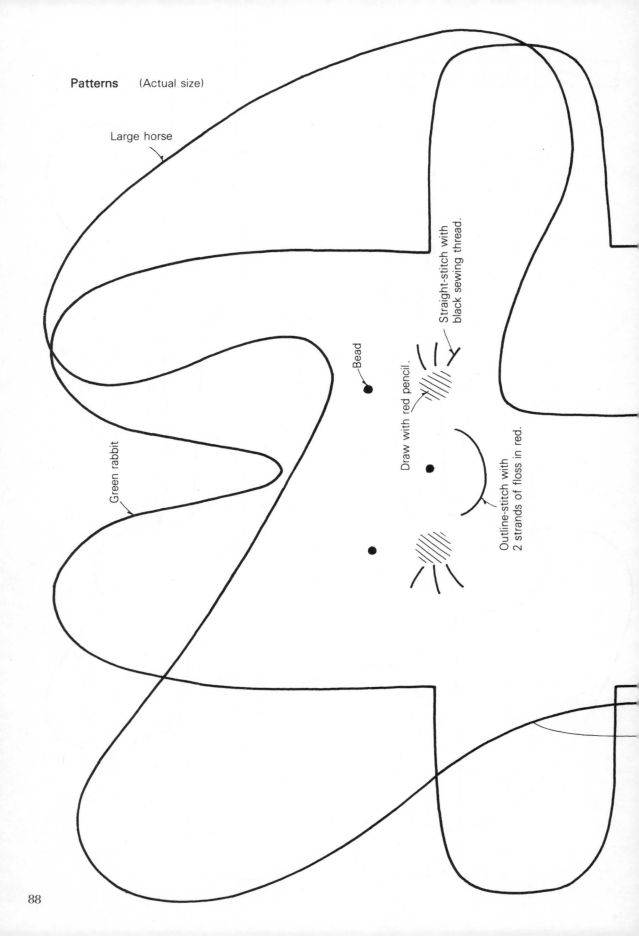

Large horse

Green rabbit

Bead

Straight-stitch with black sewing thread.

Draw with red pencil.

Outline-stitch with 2 strands of floss in red.

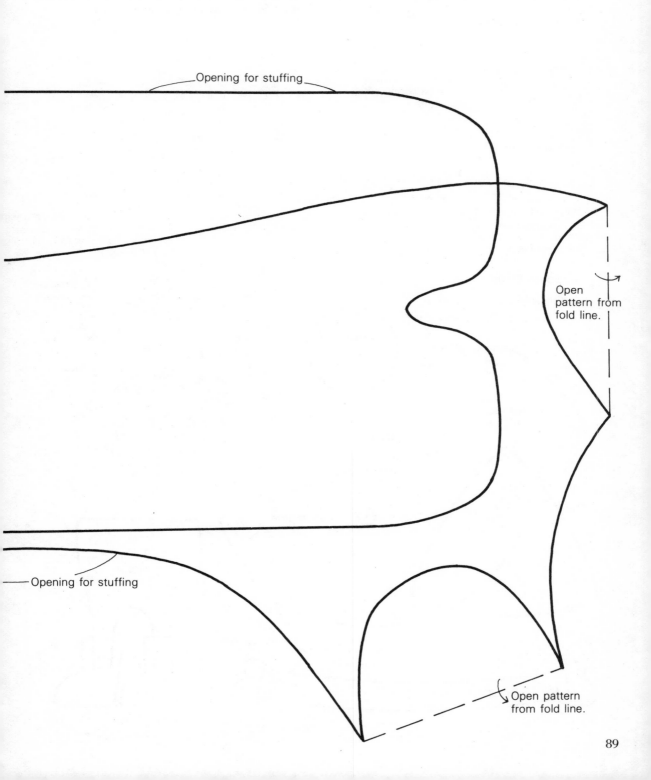

Opening for stuffing

Open
pattern from
fold line.

Opening for stuffing

Open pattern
from fold line.

MATERIALS

FABRIC: Cotton prints: 12 pieces of 8.5 cm by 16.5 cm.
Felt: Scraps of red, white, pink and black. Glue. Rouge.
Quilt batting. Polyester fiberfill. Green ribbon, 1.2 cm
by 60 cm. 70 cm wire. Round beads (small): 2 black and
1 red.
FINISHED SIZE: See diagram.

DIRECTIONS:

Make 12 puffs following diagram. Arrange puffs so that
colors harmonize. Insert wire into center of puffs using
awl and twist ends. Twist ends of wire to make hanger.
Make Santa Claus and sew on. Sew on bow.

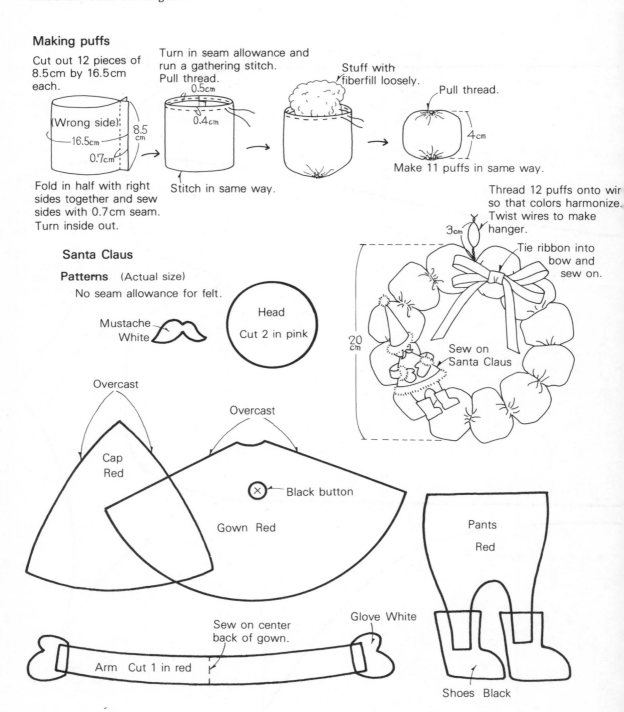

Making puffs

Cut out 12 pieces of 8.5 cm by 16.5 cm each.

(Wrong side) 16.5 cm 8.5 cm 0.7 cm

Fold in half with right sides together and sew sides with 0.7 cm seam. Turn inside out.

Turn in seam allowance and run a gathering stitch. Pull thread.

0.5 cm 0.4 cm

Stitch in same way.

Stuff with fiberfill loosely.

Pull thread. 4 cm

Make 11 puffs in same way.

Thread 12 puffs onto wire so that colors harmonize. Twist wires to make hanger.

3 cm

Tie ribbon into bow and sew on.

Santa Claus

Patterns (Actual size)

No seam allowance for felt.

Mustache White

Head Cut 2 in pink

20 cm

Sew on Santa Claus

Overcast

Cap Red

Overcast

Black button

Gown Red

Pants Red

Sew on center back of gown.

Glove White

Arm Cut 1 in red

Shoes Black

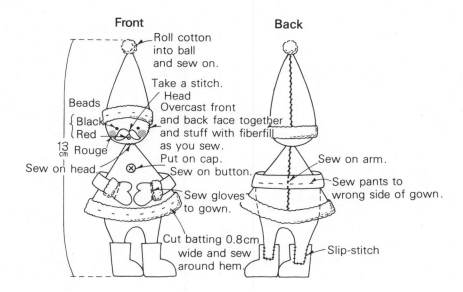

Front

Back

Roll cotton
into ball
and sew on.

Take a stitch.
Head
Overcast front
and back face together
and stuff with fiberfill
as you sew.
Put on cap.
Sew on button.

Beads
{ Black
{ Red
13
cm Rouge

Sew on head.

Sew gloves
to gown.

Cut batting 0.8cm
wide and sew
around hem.

Sew on arm.

Sew pants to
wrong side of gown.

Slip-stitch

 X'mas Pillows, shown on pages 32 & 33.

MATERIALS
FABRIC: Cotton prints: FOR PILLOW ON PAGE 32:
(a) white with design, 50cm by 30cm; (b) red with
design, 30cm square; (c) dots; (d) green with design,
25cm by 12cm each; (e) green, 42cm by 38cm. FOR
PILLOW ON PAGE 33: (a-d) same prints as above but
the following amounts: (a) 45cm square; (b) 30cm
square; (c) 24cm square; (d) 35cm square; (e) red, 42cm
by 38cm; (f) small amount of dark green. Quilt batting
and backing, 38cm square each. White quilting thread.
White embroidery floss, No. 25. 30cm zipper. 38cm-
square inner pillow stuffed with kapok.

FINISHED SIZE: 36cm square.
DIRECTIONS:
1. Cut out patches and sew them together by hand.
2. Draw quilting lines. Pin and baste top, batting and
   backing together and quilt.
3. Embroider.
4. Sew zipper to back pieces.
5. Sew front and back together with right sides facing.
   Zigzag-stitch along raw edges by machine. Turn inside out.
6. Insert inner pillow.

Embroidery patterns

(Actual size)

Chain-stitch with 3 strands of
floss in white.

Merry

X'mas

Front

Add 0.7cm seam allowance unless otherwise indicated.
Cut 37.5cm square each from batting and backing.

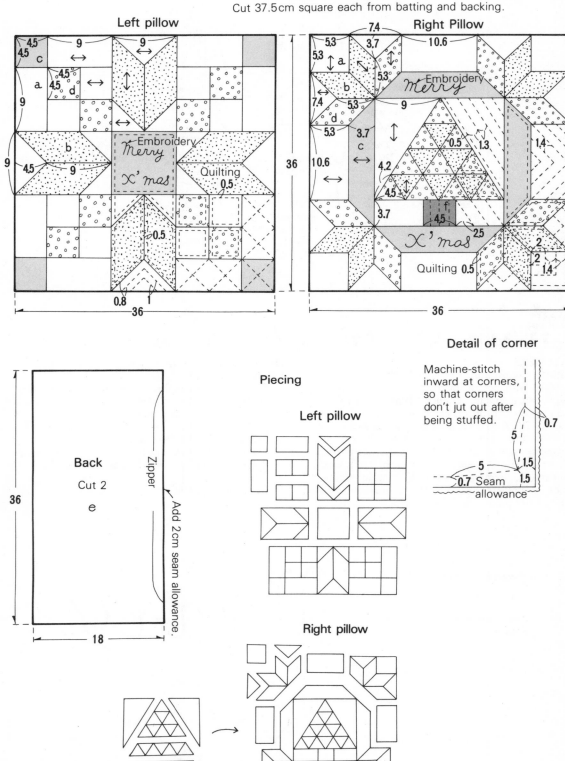

Left pillow

Right Pillow

Embroidery
Merry
X' mas

Quilting 0.5

Detail of corner

Machine-stitch inward at corners, so that corners don't jut out after being stuffed.

0.7 Seam allowance

Back

Cut 2

e

Zipper

Add 2cm seam allowance.

Piecing

Left pillow

Right pillow

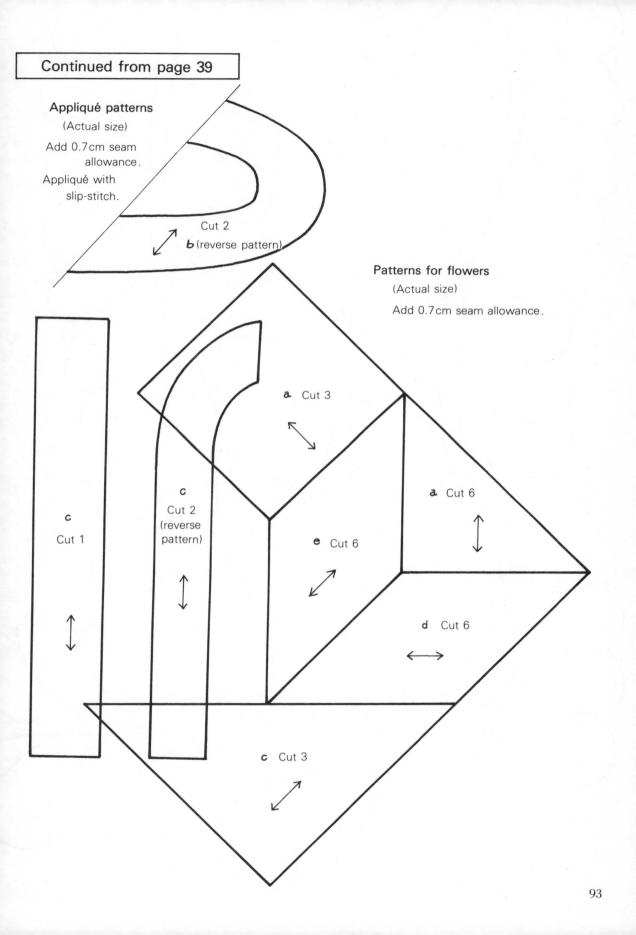

Continued from page 39

Appliqué patterns

(Actual size)

Add 0.7cm seam
allowance.

Appliqué with
slip-stitch.

Cut 2

b (reverse pattern)

Patterns for flowers

(Actual size)

Add 0.7cm seam allowance.

a Cut 3

c
Cut 2
(reverse
pattern)

c
Cut 1

a Cut 6

e Cut 6

d Cut 6

c Cut 3

Quilting patterns
(Actual size)
Stitch with white thread.

Center→

Quilting patterns

(Actual size)

Stitch with navy thread

Center

95

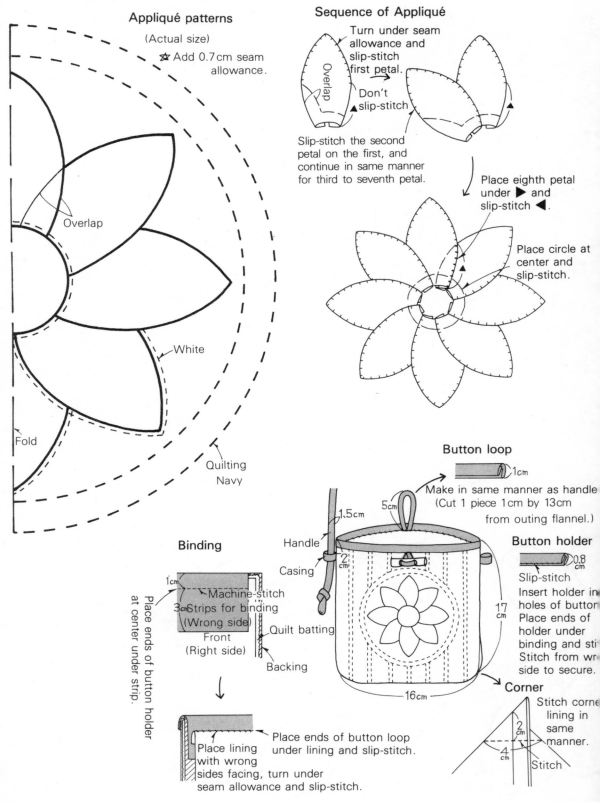

Appliqué patterns

(Actual size)

☆ Add 0.7cm seam allowance.

Overlap

White

Fold

Quilting Navy

Sequence of Appliqué

Turn under seam allowance and slip-stitch first petal.

Overlap

Don't ▲ slip-stitch

Slip-stitch the second petal on the first, and continue in same manner for third to seventh petal.

Place eighth petal under ▶ and slip-stitch ◀.

Place circle at center and slip-stitch.

Button loop

1cm

Make in same manner as handle (Cut 1 piece 1cm by 13cm from outing flannel.)

Button holder

0.8 cm

Slip-stitch

Insert holder in holes of button Place ends of holder under binding and sti Stitch from wr side to secure.

Binding

1cm
Machine-stitch
3cm Strips for binding
(Wrong side)
Front
(Right side)

Place ends of button holder at center under strip.

Quilt batting

Backing

Place lining with wrong sides facing, turn under seam allowance and slip-stitch.

Place ends of button loop under lining and slip-stitch.

1.5cm

5cm

Handle

Casing

2 cm

17 cm

16cm

Corner

Stitch corne lining in same manner.

2 cm

4 cm

Stitch

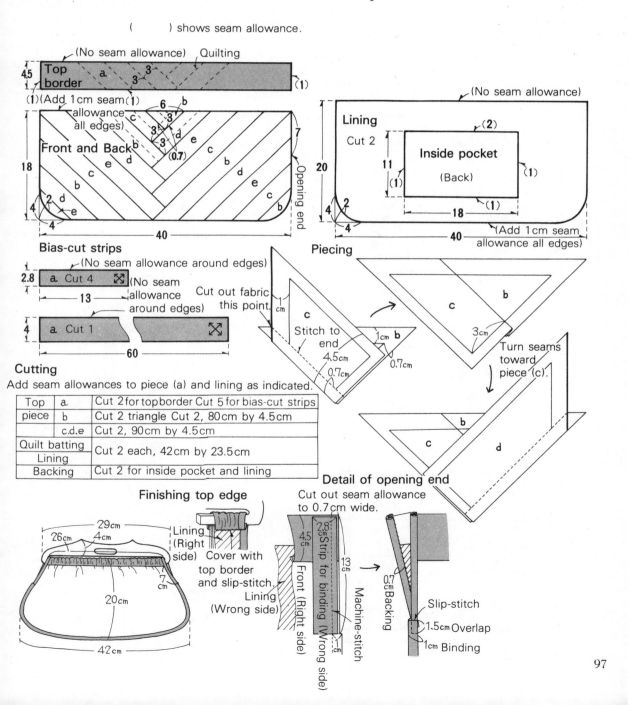

MATERIALS

FABRIC: Cotton fabric: (a) 60 cm by 45 cm (black for Black Purse and red for Red Purse); (b-e) (see photo), 90 cm by 10 cm each; for backing, 42 cm by 47 cm; for lining, 62 cm by 42 cm. Quilt batting, 42 cm by 47 cm. Quilting thread: black for Black Purse and red for Red Purse. One pair of handles, 29 cm long.

FINISHED SIZE: See diagram.

DIRECTIONS:

1. Cut out fabric following diagram. Sew patches together by hand. Make front and back.

2. Sew border to top of front and back individually. Draw quilting lines.
3. Pin and baste top, batting and backing together. Quilt.
4. Sew inside pocket to lining.
5. Pin and baste quilted piece and lining with wrong sides facing. Bind side edges.
6. With wrong sides facing, bind edges of front and back together.
7. Insert top border into handle, turn in seam allowance and slip-stitch.

( ) shows seam allowance.

Cutting

Add seam allowances to piece (a) and lining as indicated.

Top piece	a	Cut 2 for top border Cut 5 for bias-cut strips
	b	Cut 2 triangle Cut 2, 80 cm by 4.5 cm
	c.d.e	Cut 2, 90 cm by 4.5 cm
Quilt batting Lining		Cut 2 each, 42 cm by 23.5 cm
Backing		Cut 2 for inside pocket and lining

MATERIALS

FABRICS: Cotton fabric: (a) 80 cm by 32 cm (Off-white for Bag at left and Lavender for Bag at right); (b) 90 cm by 65 cm (dark brown for left Bag and purple for right Bag); (c-f) 16 cm square each; for backing, 85 cm by 32 cm; for lining, 72 cm by 50 cm. Quilt batting, 85 cm by 32 cm. Outing flannel, 90 cm by 15 cm. Quilting thread: white and brown for left Bag and white for right Bag. One 5 cm-long bamboo button. Cardboard, same size as bottom.

FINISHED SIZE: See diagram.

DIRECTIONS:

1. Cut out patches for front. Appliqué handles and sew patches together by hand.

2. Sew front, gussets and back together, following diagram. Draw quilting lines.

3. Pin and baste top, batting and backing together. Quilt diagonally. Pin and baste pieces for bottom together and quilt diagonally in two directions.

4. Sew side seams. Sew inside pocket to lining. Sew pieces of lining together in same manner.

5. With wrong sides facing, place quilted piece on lining. Bind edges of body and bottom together.

6. Make handles, button loop and button holder following directions on page 46, 47 and 96. Bind edges of opening, catching ends of handles, loop and holder.

7. Place cardboard on bottom.

(　　) shows seam allowance.
[　　] shows left bag, <　　> shows right bag and same color unless otherwise indicated.
Cut out quilt batting, lining and backing, 71.5 cm by 31.5 cm each.

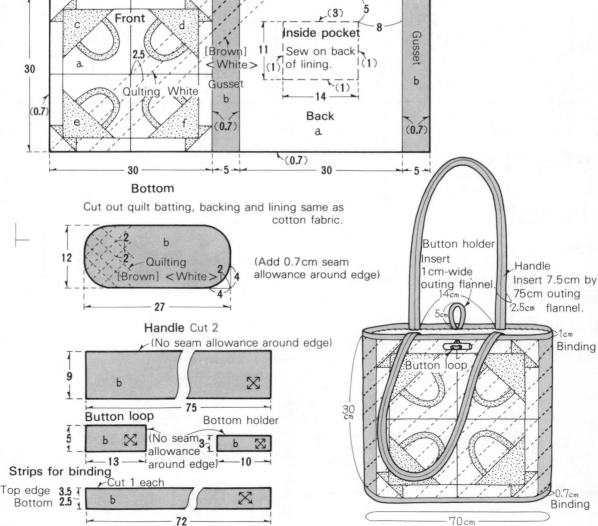

Patterns   (Actual size)   Add 0.7cm seam allowance.

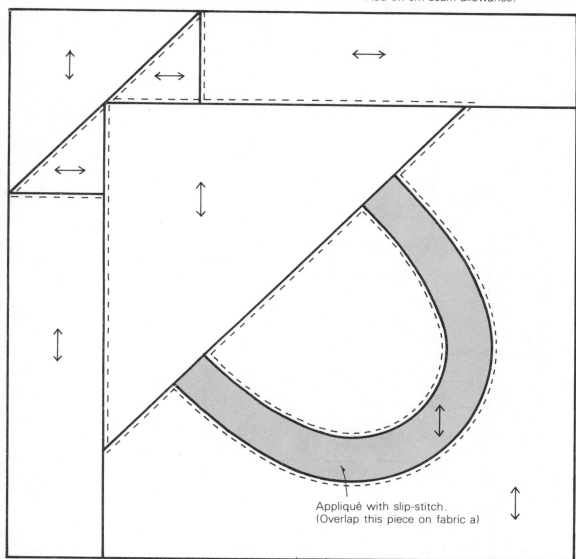

Appliqué with slip-stitch.
(Overlap this piece on fabric a)

Tea Cozy and Matching Mat,
shown on page 49.

MATERIALS
FABRIC: Cotton fabric: FOR TEA COZY: (a) red with floral design, 35 cm square; (b) red, 50 cm by 60 cm; (c) small amount of white with floral design. FOR MAT: Same as Tea Cozy: (a) 35 cm square; (b) 50 cm by 30 cm; (d) small amount. Polyester fiberfill.
FINISHED SIZE: See diagram.
DIRECTIONS FOR TEA COZY:
1. Cut patches for front and one piece of back adding seam allowance. Sew patches together by hand.

2. With wrong sides facing, sew bottom seams of top and lining. Insert fiberfill.
3. Make loop.
4. Bind edges of front and back together catching ends of loop placed on back.
FOR MAT:
1. Work same as Tea Cozy.
2. Place fiberfill thinly between top and lining. Bind edges.

Patterns (Actual size) · Add 0.7 cm seam allowance.

Tea cozy.....Top piece (Patchwork), Lining (Fabirc b).....Cut 2 each.

Mat.....Top piece (Patchwork), Lining (Fabric a).....Cut 1 each.

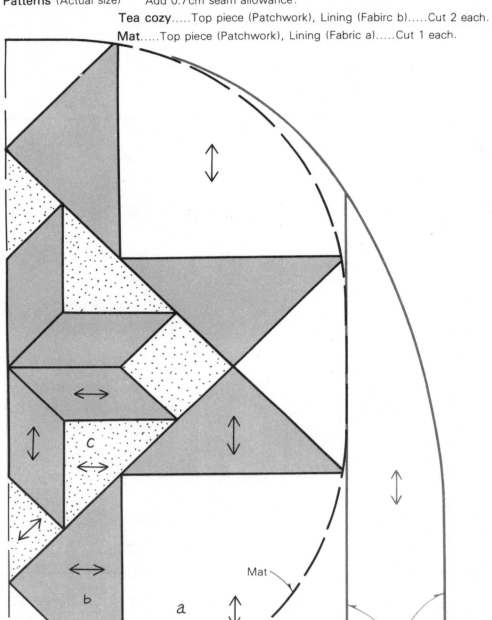

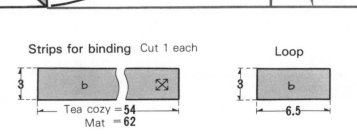

Strips for binding Cut 1 each

3

b

Tea cozy = **54**
Mat = **62**

Loop

3

b

6.5

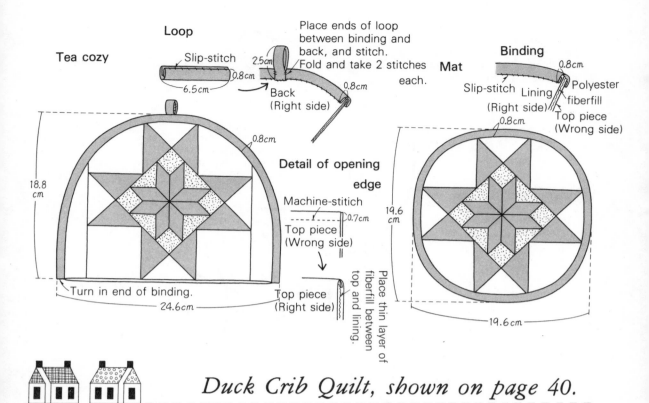

Tea cozy

Loop

Slip-stitch

6.5cm   0.8cm   2.5cm

Place ends of loop
between binding and
back, and stitch.
Fold and take 2 stitches
each.

Back
(Right side)

0.8cm

Mat

Binding

0.8cm

Slip-stitch   Lining   Polyester
(Right side)   fiberfill
Top piece
(Wrong side)

0.8cm

18.8
cm

0.8cm

**Detail of opening
edge**

Machine-stitch

0.7cm

Top piece
(Wrong side)

Top piece
(Right side)

19.6
cm

Turn in end of binding.

24.6cm

Place thin layer of
fiberfill between
top and lining.

19.6cm

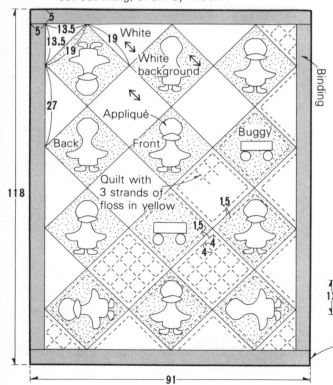

Duck Crib Quilt, shown on page 40.

Add 1 cm seam allowance to patches.
Fold quilt batting in half to make 120cm by 92.5cm.
Fold excess when binding.

Cut out lining, 91 cm by 118cm.

5
5   13.5
13.5   19
19

White

White
background

Appliqué

27

Back   Front

Buggy

Quilt with
3 strands of
floss in yellow

Binding

1.5

1.5

4
4

118

91

See page 2 for
finishing corners.

MATERIALS
FABRICS: Cotton broadcloth: White, 90cm
square; white with small flowers, 85cm by
65cm; yellow with small flowers, 50cm by
110cm; for lining, 91cm by 118cm. Cotton
fabric for appliques: Light yellow, 75cm by
40cm; orange, 30cm square; small amount of
blue. Quilt batting, 120cm by 185cm. Embroidery floss, No. 25: 2 skeins of yellow and
small amount of charcoal gray.
FINISHED SIZE: 118cm by 91cm.
DIRECTIONS:
1. Cut patches adding 1cm seam allowance
and sew them together by machine.
2. Cut appliques adding 0.7cm seam
allowance. Appliqué in place using slip-
stitch.

Strips for binding

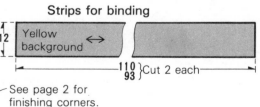

12

Yellow
background

110
93   Cut 2 each

101

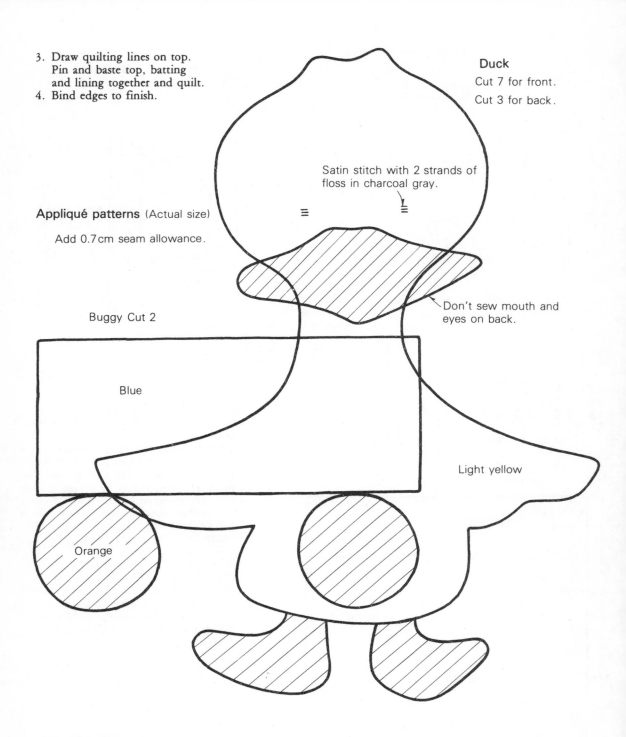

3. Draw quilting lines on top.
   Pin and baste top, batting
   and lining together and quilt.
4. Bind edges to finish.

Duck

Cut 7 for front.

Cut 3 for back.

Satin stitch with 2 strands of
floss in charcoal gray.

Appliqué patterns (Actual size)

Add 0.7 cm seam allowance.

Don't sew mouth and
eyes on back.

Buggy Cut 2

Blue

Light yellow

Orange

Potholders, shown on page 53.

OCTAGON
MATERIALS
FABRICS: Cotton fabric: Brick red, 30 cm square;
unbleached, 25 cm square; green, 10 cm by 20 cm; green
and white stripes, 12 cm by 22 cm; backing, 18 cm square.

Outing flannel, 36 cm by 18 cm. Dark brown quilting
thread.
FINISHED SIZE: See diagram.
DIRECTIONS: Make in same manner as Potholders on
page 54.

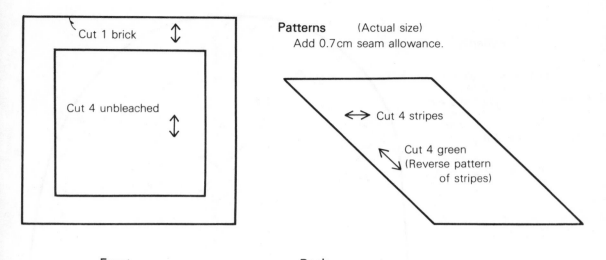

Cut 1 brick

Patterns (Actual size)
Add 0.7 cm seam allowance.

Cut 4 unbleached

↔ Cut 4 stripes

Cut 4 green
(Reverse pattern
of stripes)

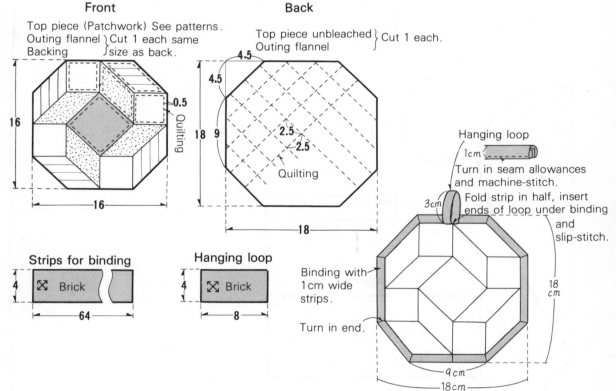

Front

Top piece (Patchwork) See patterns.
Outing flannel } Cut 1 each same
Backing } size as back.

16

16

0.5

Quilting

Back

Top piece unbleached } Cut 1 each.
Outing flannel

4.5

4.5

18 9

2.5

2.5

Quilting

18

Hanging loop

1cm

Turn in seam allowances
and machine-stitch.

Fold strip in half, insert
ends of loop under binding
and
slip-stitch.

3cm

Binding with
1cm wide
strips.

Turn in end.

18 cm

9 cm

18cm

Strips for binding

⊠ Brick

4

64

Hanging loop

⊠ Brick

4

8

MITTEN
MATERIALS
FABRICS: Cotton fabric: Red with yellow stars, 45 cm
by 40 cm; small amount each of unbleached, mustard,
and green; for lining, 40 cm by 24 cm. Outing flannel,
60 cm by 24 cm. Red sewing thread.
FINISHED SIZE: See diagram.
DIRECTIONS:
1. Place one piece of outing flannel between top and

lining of front and place two pieces of outing flannel for back. Pin and baste. Quilt by machine.
2. Sew patches together following directions on page 105
and machine-stitch patches to front with tapes.
3. With right sides facing, sew front and back together.
Overcast raw edges to prevent fraying.
4. Turn inside out. Bind edges of opening, catching ends
of loop.

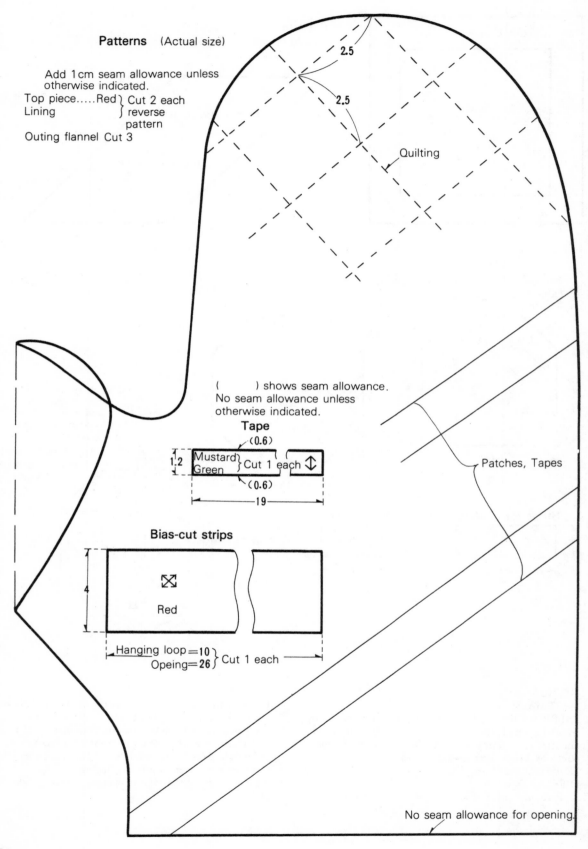

Patterns (Actual size)

Add 1cm seam allowance unless otherwise indicated.

Top piece.....Red } Cut 2 each
Lining } reverse pattern
Outing flannel Cut 3

2.5

2.5

Quilting

( ) shows seam allowance.
No seam allowance unless otherwise indicated.

Tape

(0.6)

1.2 Mustard } Cut 1 each ⇕
Green

(0.6)

19

Patches, Tapes

Bias-cut strips

4

⊠

Red

Hanging loop=10 } Cut 1 each
Opeing=26

No seam allowance for opening.

104

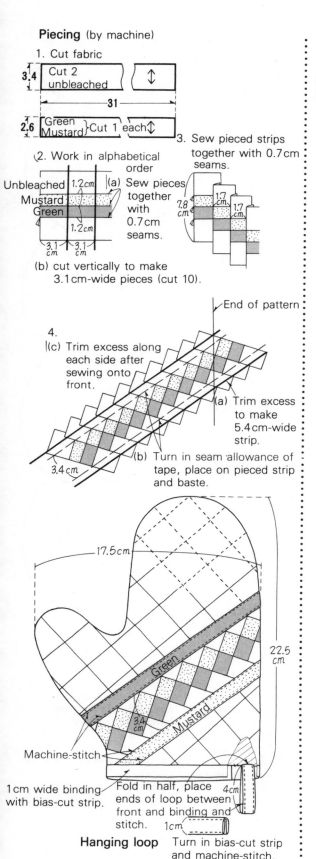

Piecing (by machine)

1. Cut fabric

3.4 | Cut 2 unbleached | ↕

31

2.6 | Green / Mustard | Cut 1 each ↕

2. Work in alphabetical order

Unbleached | 1.2cm | (a) Sew pieces together with 0.7cm seams.
Mustard
Green

1.2cm

3.1 cm | 3.1 cm

(b) cut vertically to make 3.1cm-wide pieces (cut 10).

3. Sew pieced strips together with 0.7cm seams.

7.8 cm | 1.7 cm | 1.7 cm

4.

(c) Trim excess along each side after sewing onto front.

End of pattern

(a) Trim excess to make 5.4cm-wide strip.

(b) Turn in seam allowance of tape, place on pieced strip and baste.

3.4 cm

17.5 cm

Green

Mustard

22.5 cm

3.4 cm

Machine-stitch

1cm wide binding with bias-cut strip.

Fold in half, place ends of loop between front and binding and stitch. 1cm

4cm

Hanging loop Turn in bias-cut strip and machine-stitch.

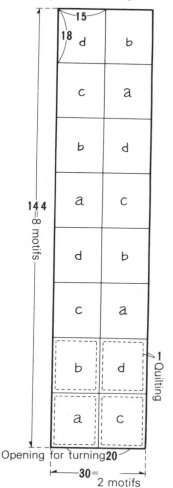

Muffler, shown on pages 60 & 61.

MATERIALS
FABRICS: Wool; (a-b) 34cm by 40cm each. Fabric for lining, 32cm by 146cm. White quilting thread.
FINISHED SIZE: 30cm by 144cm.
DIRECTIONS:
1. Cut out patches and sew them together by machine.
2. With right sides facing, sew pieced top and lining together, leaving opening for turning. Turn inside out and slip-stitch opening closed.
3. Quilt along seams of each patch.

Add 1cm seam allowance.

Cut out lining, 32cm by 146cm.

15

18 | d | b

c | a

b | d

144 = 8 motifs | a | c

d | b

c | a

b | d

1 Quilting

a | c

Opening for turning 20

30 = 2 motifs

Continued from page 59

Quilting patterns

(Actual size)

Pattern of border
strip corners.

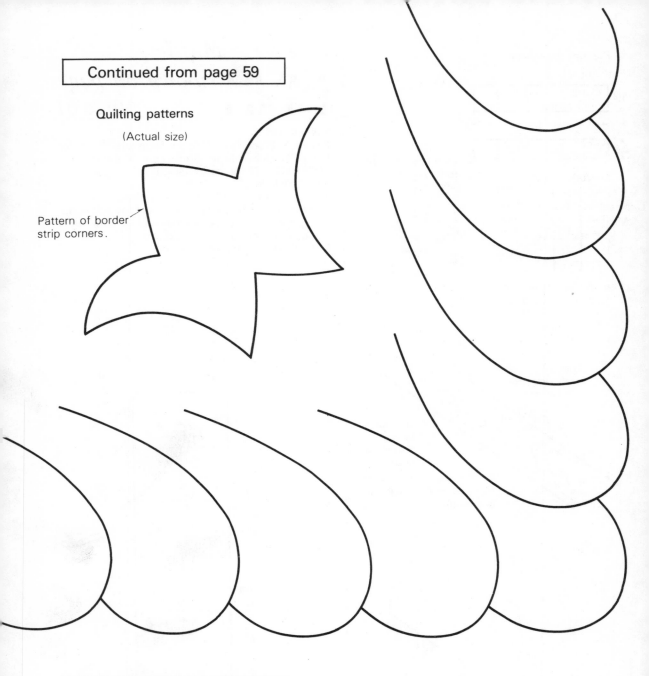

Continued from page 63

Child's Happi Coat
MATERIALS
FABRICS: Cotton fabric: (g) pink, 90 cm square; (h) rose pink, 50 cm by 40 cm; (a-f) small amount of each. Fabrics for backing and lining, 90 cm square each. Quilt batting, 90 cm square. Red quilting thread. Embroidery floss, No. 25: purple and blue.
FINISHED SIZE: Width across back, 42 cm. Length, 44 cm. Sleeve length from center back, 38 cm.
DIRECTIONS:
1. Cut out pieces from fabrics and batting.

2. Cut out appliques. Appliqué leaves on front. Make 10 pieces of yo-yo flowers and sew in place.
3. Sew center back seams of top and lining individually. Press seams open.
4. Draw quilting lines on top. Pin and baste top, batting and backing together. Quilt.
5. Quilt along leaves. Embroider.
6. Make in same manner as Mother's Happi Coat for 10—12 on page 63.

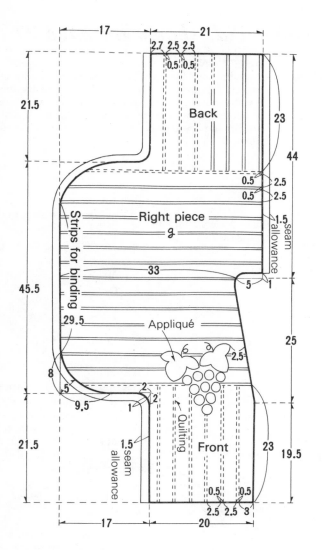

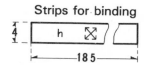

Cut out left piece (reverse pattern)

Cut one left and right quilt batting and backing as one continuous piece without seam allowance at center back.
Cut lining same size as top piece.

Strips for binding

h

18.5

Grape

(Yo-yo)

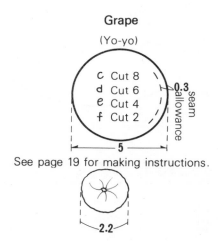

c Cut 8
d Cut 6
e Cut 4
f Cut 2

0.3 seam allowance

5

See page 19 for making instructions.

2.2

Appliqué patterns (Actual size)   Add 0.5cm seam allowance. **Leave** Cut 2 each.

Quilt along appliqué.   Outline stitch with 2 strands of floss. (Cut out other one by reverse pattern)

Purple
Blue

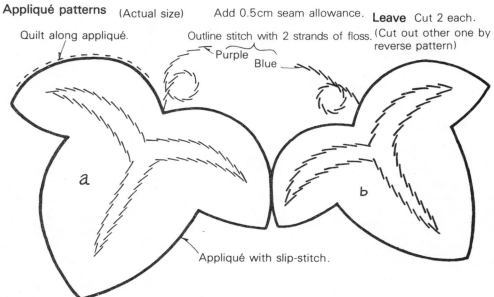

a

b

Appliqué with slip-stitch.

MATERIALS

FABRICS: Cotton broadcloth: Off-white with wild berries, 90cm by 50cm; off-white, 90cm by 36cm; brown, 90cm by 10cm. Quilt batting, 31cm by 25cm. Outing flannel, 90cm by 12cm. Brown embroidery floss, No.25. Elastic tape, 1.4cm by 40cm. Cardboard, 31cm by 25cm.

FINISHED SIZE: See diagram.

DIRECTIONS:

Cut fabrics and batting. Pin and baste top, batting and backing together. Appliqué on top, catching backing. Sew bias-cut strip to edges. Place cardboard and lining on backing. Bind edges of all pieces in slip-stitch. Make handles and sew in place. Braid tapes and sew on in slip stitch.

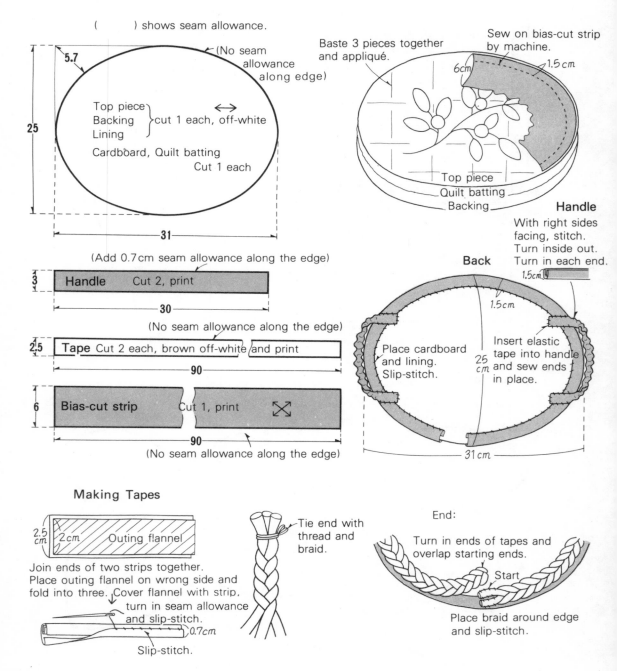

( ) shows seam allowance.

5.7

(No seam allowance along edge)

25

Top piece
Backing
Lining
}cut 1 each, off-white

Cardboard, Quilt batting
Cut 1 each

31

(Add 0.7cm seam allowance along the edge)

3 | **Handle** Cut 2, print
30

(No seam allowance along the edge)

2.5 | **Tape** Cut 2 each, brown off-white and print
90

6 | **Bias-cut strip** Cut 1, print
90

(No seam allowance along the edge)

Baste 3 pieces together and appliqué.

Sew on bias-cut strip by machine.

6cm

1.5 cm

Top piece
Quilt batting
Backing

Handle
With right sides facing, stitch. Turn inside out. Turn in each end.

1.5cm

Back

1.5 cm

1.5 cm

Place cardboard and lining. Slip-stitch.

25 cm

Insert elastic tape into handle and sew ends in place.

31cm

Making Tapes

2.5 cm | 2cm Outing flannel

Join ends of two strips together. Place outing flannel on wrong side and fold into three. Cover flannel with strip, turn in seam allowance and slip-stitch.

0.7cm

Slip-stitch.

Tie end with thread and braid.

End:

Turn in ends of tapes and overlap starting ends.

Start

Place braid around edge and slip-stitch.

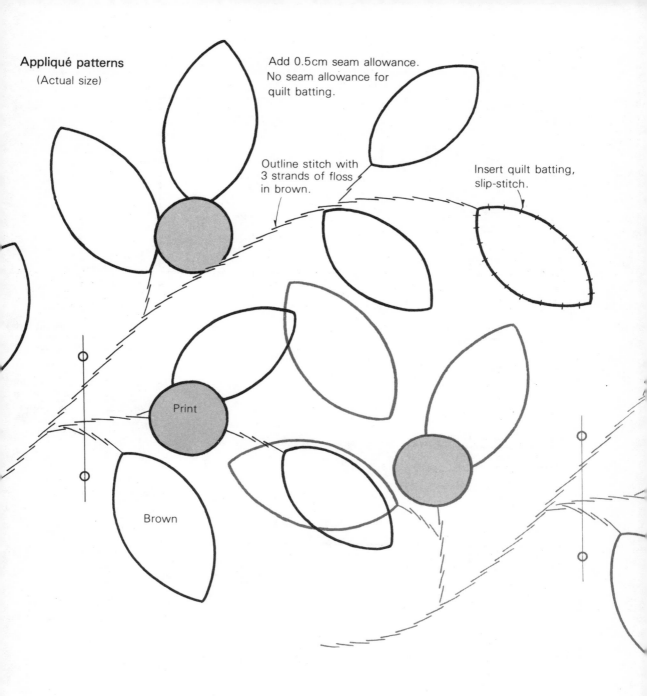

Appliqué patterns
(Actual size)

Add 0.5cm seam allowance.
No seam allowance for
quilt batting.

Outline stitch with
3 strands of floss
in brown.

Insert quilt batting,
slip-stitch.

Print

Brown

  Cosmetic Cases, shown on pages 68 & 69.

MATERIALS (FOR ONE)
FABRIC: Cotton fabric: Off-white, 45 cm by 25 cm; small amount each of 5 different prints and solids (see photo); for lining, 19 cm by 37.5 cm. Quilt batting, 19.5 cm by 37.5 cm. White quilting thread. 18 cm zipper for B. One button, 1.5 cm in diameter for C.
FINISHED SIZE: See diagram.

DIRECTIONS:
1. Cut fabric. Appliqué stem. Sew patches together by hand.
2. Sew bottom seams of front and back. Draw quilting lines. Pin and baste top and batting. Quilt.
3. Sew side seams with right sides together. Sew side seams of lining. Sew corners of bottom for B. Finish following diagrams on next page.

Add 0.7cm seam allowance unless otherwise indicated.
Cut out 1 piece of quilt batting, 19.5cm by 37.4cm.
Cut out 1 piece of lining, 19cm by 37.4cm.

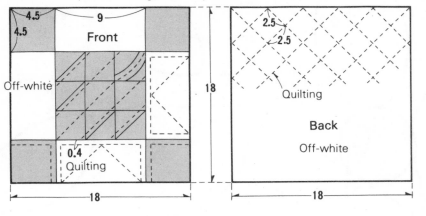

4.5
4.5
9
Front
Off-white
18
0.4
Quilting
18

2.5
2.5
Quilting
Back
Off-white
18

Strips for binding

(No seam allowance along edge)

2.8
Off-white
↕
38

Button loop of C

(No seam allowance along edge)

2
Off-white
↕
10

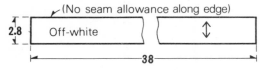

Patterns (Actual size)

Add 0.7cm seam allowance.

Appliqué with slip-stitch

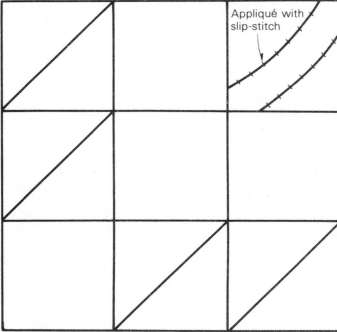

Opening

With right sides together, stitch.

Strip for binding (Wrong side)

Front (Right side)

Place zipper on
0.7cm right side of strip and sew on with back stitch
0.7cm

Slip-stitch
Lining
(Right side)
(Wrong side)

B

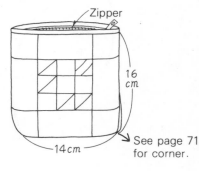

Zipper

16
cm

14cm

See page 71 for corner.

C: See page 71 for opening and button loop.

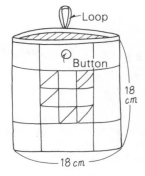

Loop

Button

18
cm

18cm

Pen Case, shown on pages 68 & 69.

MATERIALS
FABRIC: Blue-gray, 16 cm by 40 cm; print, 35 cm square; for lining, 9 cm by 40 cm. Quilt batting, 9 cm by 40 cm. White quilting thread. One snap fastener.
FINISHED SIZE: See diagram.
DIRECTIONS:
1. Cut fabric. Sew patches together by hand.
2. Draw quilting lines on top. Pin and baste top, batting and lining together. Quilt.
3. Bind straight edges. Fold in half with wrong sides together. Bind edges all around except bottom.
4. Sew on snap fastener.

Add 0.7 cm seam allowance.
Cut quilt batting and lining same size as top piece.

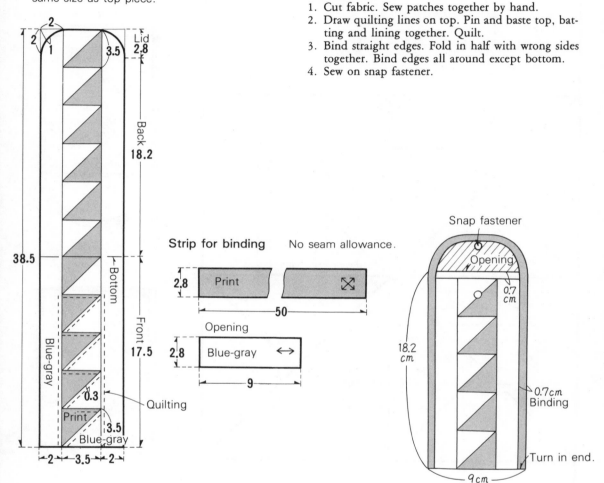

Glasses Case, shown on page 69.

MATERIALS
FABRIC: Cotton fabric: Dotted print, 40 cm by 20 cm; beige, 40 cm square; small amount each of 8 different prints and solids for patches (see photo). Quilt batting, 23 cm by 20 cm. White quilting thread.
FINISHED SIZE: 11.5 cm by 19.5 cm.

DIRECTIONS:
1. Cut fabric. Sew patches together by hand.
2. Draw quilting lines on front and back. Pin and baste front, batting and lining together. Baste back pieces in same manner. Quilt.
3. Bind top edges of front and back individually. With wrong sides facing, bind edges of front and back together.

111

Front   (Actual size)

Add 0.7 cm seam allowance.

Cut 1 piece of back same size as front in dotted print.
Cut 2 pieces each of quilt batting and lining (beige) same size as front.

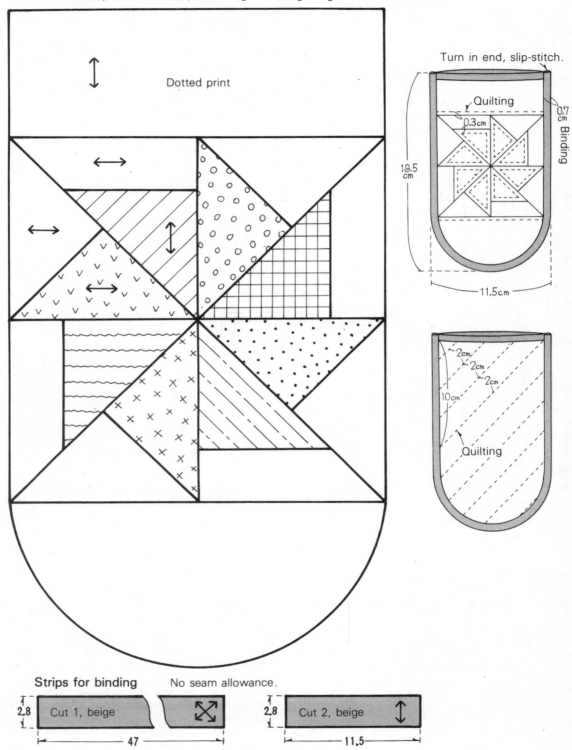

Strips for binding   No seam allowance.

MATERIALS

FABRICS: Blue quilted fabric, 23 cm square. Cotton fabric: For appliques, small amount each of 9 different prints and solids; for lining, 23 cm square. White cotton lace edging (gathered), 2.5 cm by 20 cm.

FINISHED SIZE: 7 cm by 21 cm.

DIRECTIONS:

1. Cut fabric. Sew patches together. Appliqué in place.
2. Sew front and back together with right sides facing. Turn inside out. Sew lining in same manner.
3. Insert lining into quilted case with wrong sides together. Place lace edging between top and lining and slip-stitch.

Patterns

(Actual size)

Add 1 cm seam allowance.
Add 0.7 cm seam allowance for appliqué fabric.

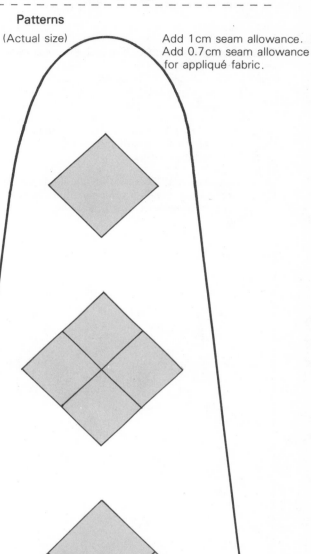

Appliqué with slip-stitch to front.

Quilting fabric ⎫
Lining ⎭ Cut 2 each

Opening

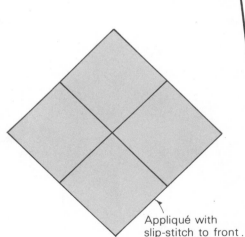

Top piece (Right side)
(b) Slip-stitch.
Lining (Wrong side)
(c) Slip-stitch
2 cm

(a) Join ends of lace edging. Place between top and lining.

ANGEL
MATERIALS

FABRIC: Cotton fabric: Small amount each of red with white dots and white with red flowers. White felt, 15 cm square. White mohair yarn (extra fine). Red ribbon, 1 cm by 35 cm. Silver spangles: 14 round and 1 star-shaped (large). Round beads: 2 black (medium) and 1 red (small). 15 transparent beads. White cotton lace edging, 1 cm by 25 cm. Polyester fiberfill. Iron-on interfacing. Rouge. Green felt-tipped pen. Glue.

FINISHED SIZE: 12 cm tall.

DIRECTIONS:

1. Cut fabric and felt. Overcast front and back of body together leaving opening for stuffing. Stuff with fiberfill. Slip-stitch opening closed. Make head in same manner.

2. Attach hair to head. Make features.
3. Sew dress.
4. Put dress on body. Sew head to body.
5. Sew 2 pieces of wing together and turn inside out. Stuff with fiberfill and slip-stitch opening closed. Make another wing in same manner.
6. Sew wings to body catching ends of ribbon.
7. Sew bow onto head. Color feet with felt-tip pen for shoes.

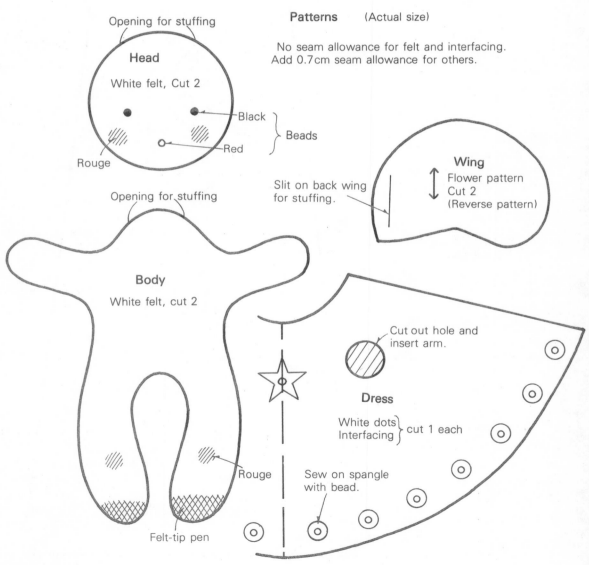

Patterns   (Actual size)

No seam allowance for felt and interfacing.
Add 0.7 cm seam allowance for others.

Opening for stuffing

Head

White felt, Cut 2

Black
Red
} Beads

Rouge

Wing
Flower pattern
Cut 2
(Reverse pattern)

Slit on back wing
for stuffing.

Opening for stuffing

Body

White felt, cut 2

Cut out hole and
insert arm.

Dress

White dots
Interfacing
} cut 1 each

Sew on spangle
with bead.

Rouge

Felt-tip pen

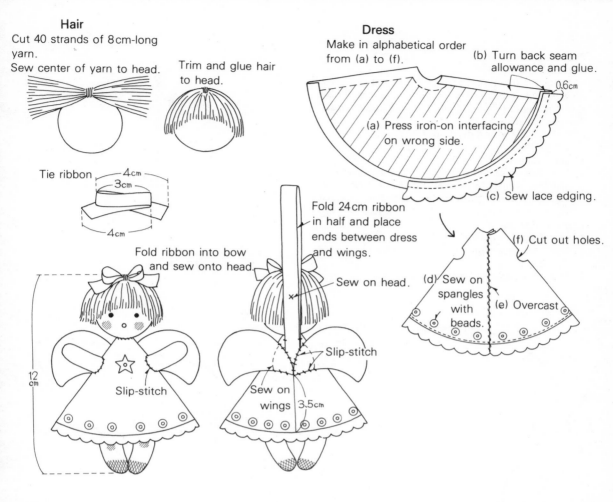

Hair

Cut 40 strands of 8cm-long yarn.

Sew center of yarn to head.

Trim and glue hair to head.

Tie ribbon — 4cm — 3cm — 4cm —

Fold ribbon into bow and sew onto head.

12 cm

Slip-stitch

Dress

Make in alphabetical order from (a) to (f).

(a) Press iron-on interfacing on wrong side.

(b) Turn back seam allowance and glue.

0.6cm

(c) Sew lace edging.

(f) Cut out holes.

(d) Sew on spangles with beads.

(e) Overcast

Fold 24cm ribbon in half and place ends between dress and wings.

Sew on head.

Slip-stitch

Sew on wings 3.5cm

BALL
MATERIALS

FABRIC: Small amount each of 4 different prints. Red ribbon, 1cm by 40cm. Polyester fiberfill.

FINISHED SIZE: 8cm in diameter.

DIRECTIONS:

1. Cut fabric. Sew 3 patches together by hand. Then sew 4 groups of 3 patches together to form ball leaving opening for stuffing.

2. Stuff with fiberfill and slip-stitch opening closed. Sew on bow.

Make 4 groups of 3 patches. Sew them together to form ball being careful not to place same design side by side and leaving opening for stuffing.

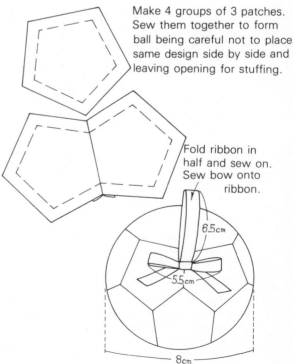

Fold ribbon in half and sew on. Sew bow onto ribbon.

6.5cm

5.5cm

8cm

Patterns (Actual size)

Add 0.7cm seam allowance.

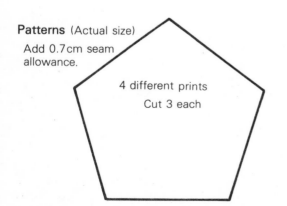

4 different prints

Cut 3 each

BIRD
MATERIALS
FABRIC: Small amount each of 2 different prints (see photo). Yellow felt. Red ribbon, 1 cm by 17 cm. 2 black round spangles (small). 2 white round beads (small). Polyester fiberfill.

FINISHED SIZE: See diagram.

DIRECTIONS:
1. Cut fabric.
2. Sew body and tail together. Sew front and back together with right sides facing and with beak and ends of ribbon in between, leaving opening for stuffing. Turn inside out. Stuff with fiberfill and slip-stitch opening closed.
3. Sew 2 pieces of wing together with right sides facing. Turn inside out. Stuff with fiberfill and slip-stitch slit closed.
4. Sew on wings and spangles with beads.

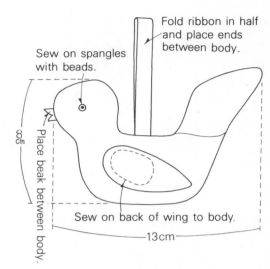

Fold ribbon in half and place ends between body.

Sew on spangles with beads.

Place beak between body.

8 cm

Sew on back of wing to body.

13 cm

Patterns (Actual size)

Add 0.7 cm seam allowance unless otherwise indicated.
Cut 2 pieces of body in reverse pattern.

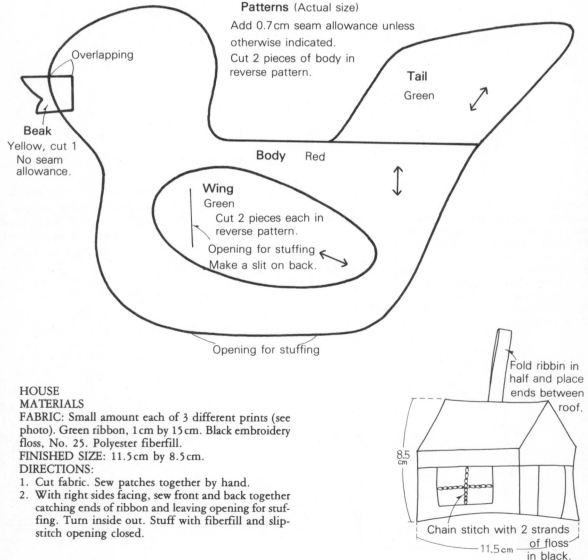

Overlapping

Tail
Green

Beak
Yellow, cut 1
No seam allowance.

Body   Red

Wing
Green
Cut 2 pieces each in reverse pattern.
Opening for stuffing
Make a slit on back.

Opening for stuffing

HOUSE
MATERIALS
FABRIC: Small amount each of 3 different prints (see photo). Green ribbon, 1 cm by 15 cm. Black embroidery floss, No. 25. Polyester fiberfill.

FINISHED SIZE: 11.5 cm by 8.5 cm.

DIRECTIONS:
1. Cut fabric. Sew patches together by hand.
2. With right sides facing, sew front and back together catching ends of ribbon and leaving opening for stuffing. Turn inside out. Stuff with fiberfill and slip-stitch opening closed.

Fold ribbin in half and place ends between roof.

8.5 cm

Chain stitch with 2 strands of floss in black.

11.5 cm

116

Patterns (Actual size)

Add 0.7 cm seam allowance.

Cut out back same size as front.

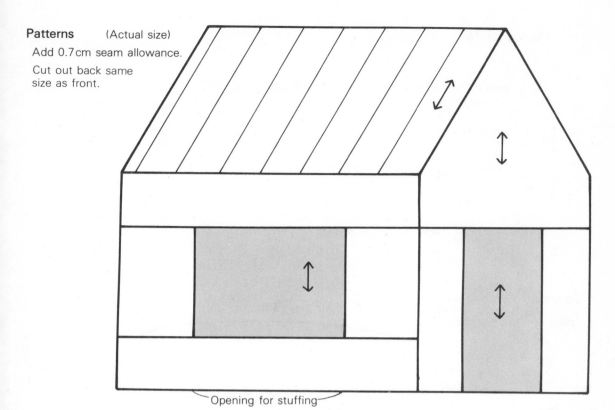

Opening for stuffing

 ## Electric Cooker Cover,
shown on page 53.

MATERIALS

FABRICS: Mustard quilted fabric, 90 cm by 29 cm. Cotton fabric: 30 cm square each of (a) white and dark brown stripes, (b) dark brown with flowers, (c) moss green with white dots and mustard; 25 cm each of red with yellow stars and unbleached; for backing, 30 cm square. Quilt batting, 30 cm square. Dark brown binding tape, 92 cm long. White quilting thread.

FINISHED SIZE: See diagram.

DIRECTIONS:

1. Cut out patches for top adding seam allowance. Sew them together by hand. Press seams following diagram on next page.
2. Pin and baste top, batting and backing together. Quilt.
3. Cut out patches for side adding seam allowance. Sew them together by hand.
4. Zigzag-stitch raw edges of side by machine. Sew side seams. Turn in seam allowance of bottom and sew together with right sides facing and binding tape in between. Zigzag-stitch raw edges.

Top

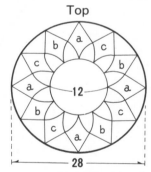

Cut out backing and quilt batting, 30 cm in diameter.

Side

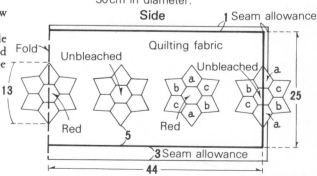

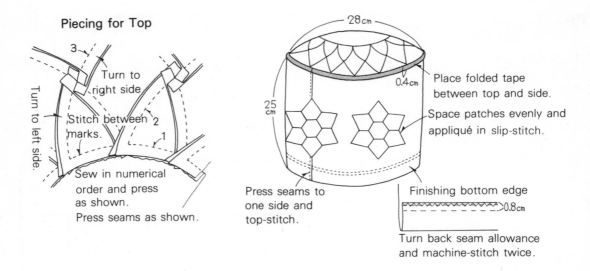

Piecing for Top

3

Turn to right side.

Turn to left side.

Stitch between marks.

2

1

Sew in numerical order and press as shown.
Press seams as shown.

28cm

0.4cm

25cm

Place folded tape between top and side.

Space patches evenly and appliqué in slip-stitch.

Press seams to one side and top-stitch.

Finishing bottom edge

0.8cm

Turn back seam allowance and machine-stitch twice.

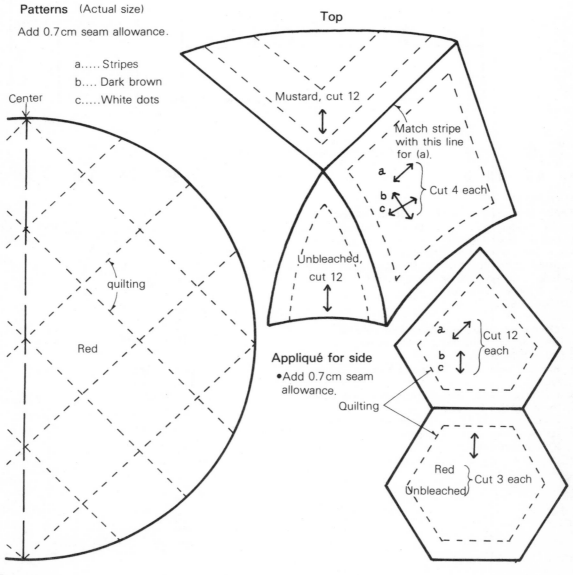

Patterns (Actual size)

Add 0.7cm seam allowance.

a.....Stripes
b....Dark brown
c.....White dots

Center

quilting

Red

Top

Mustard, cut 12

Match stripe with this line for (a).

a
b
c
} Cut 4 each

Unbleached, cut 12

Appliqué for side

• Add 0.7cm seam allowance.

Quilting

a
b
c
} Cut 12 each

Red
Unbleached
} Cut 3 each

MATERIALS

FABRICS: Mustard quilted fabric, 70 cm by 65 cm. Cotton fabric: Red with yellow stars, 55 cm by 25 cm; dark brown with white dots and unbleached, 55 cm by 20 cm each.

FINISHED SIZE: See diagram.

DIRECTIONS:

1. Sew patches together. Sew pieced patches onto front and back with tapes.

2. Appliqué 3 patches on top. Zigzag-stitch raw edges by machine.

3. Bind top edge of pocket. Tie ribbon into bow and sew onto pocket.

4. Sew bottom of pocket onto gusset. Zigzag-stitch raw edges.

5. Sew gussets, front and back together with right sides facing. Turn back seam allowance of bottom and machine-stitch.

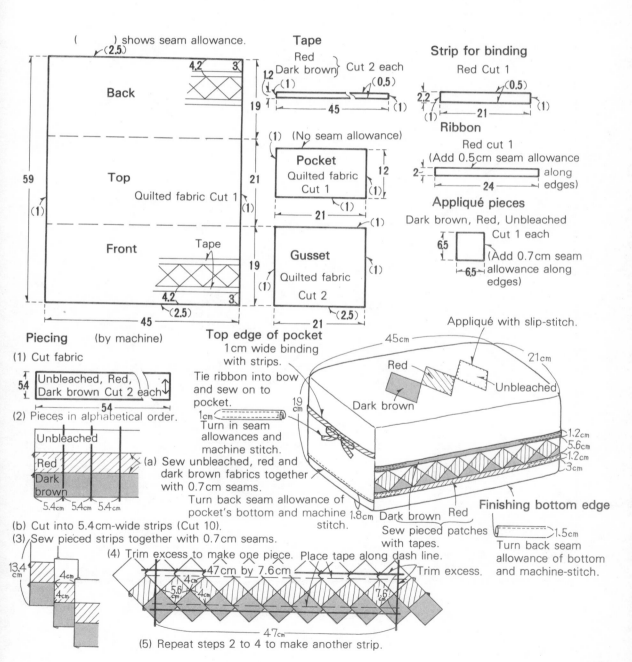

Sewing Box, shown on page 72.

MATERIALS

FABRIC: Cotton broadcloth: (a-k) Small amount each of 11 different prints and solids (see photo). Empty box, 23.5 cm by 15.5 cm by 6.7 cm. Quilt batting, 23.5 cm by 15.5 cm. Heavy-duty white cotton sewing thread for quilting. white cotton lace edging (gathered), 2.5 cm by 80 cm. Gray thick paper. Glue.

DIRECTIONS:

1. Cut out patches and background fabric for lid. Sew patches together by hand.
2. Appliqué pieced patches to foundation blocks with running stitch. Sew blocks together by hand. Pin and baste top and batting together. Quilt along seams of center square. Bind edges.

Lid   (Actual size)

No seam allowance along edges. Cut out adding 0.5 cm seam allowance unless edges.
Cut out background fabric (a ~ c) continuing shaded part.
Quilt batting 23.5 × 15.5 cm

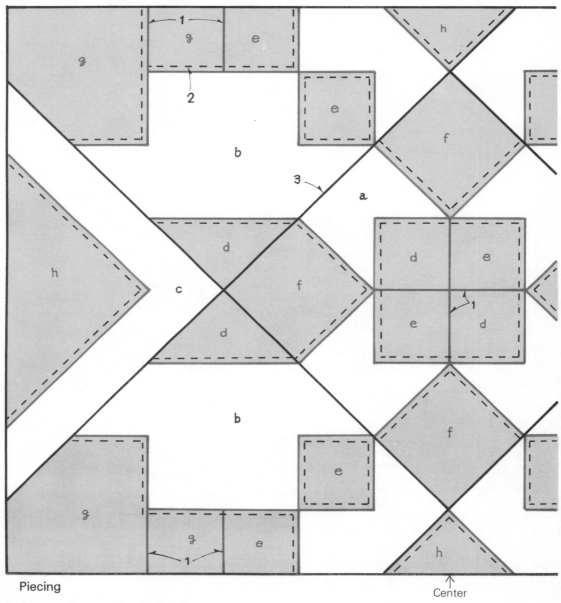

Piecing

1. Sew patches together by hand.

2. Appliqué pieced patches (d ~ h) to foundation blocks (a ~ c) with running stitch.

3. Sew blocks together by hand.

3. Glue lace edging around lid. Glue quilted top onto lid.
4. Cut out pieces for sides. Sew them together alternating 2 different prints. Sew side seams.

5. Glue pieced sides onto box.

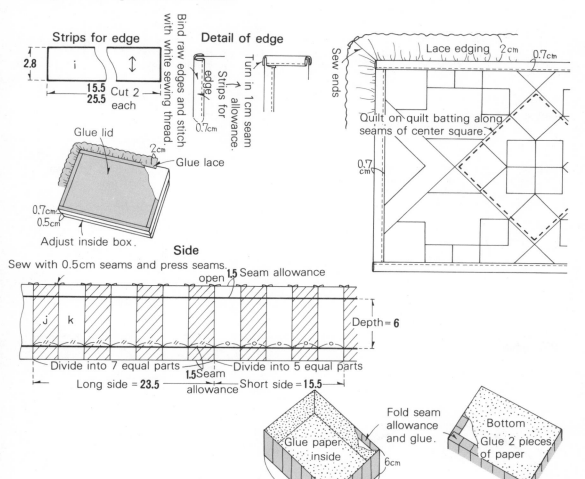

Strips for edge

2.8

i

15.5
25.5 Cut 2 each

Bind raw edges and stitch with white sewing thread.

Detail of edge

Turn in 1cm seam allowance.

Strips for edge

0.7cm

Glue lid

2cm

Glue lace

0.7cm
0.5cm

Adjust inside box.

Lace edging   2cm   0.7cm

Sew ends

Quilt on quilt batting along seams of center square.

0.7 cm

Side

Sew with 0.5cm seams and press seams.

open 1.5 Seam allowance

j   k

Depth = 6

Divide into 7 equal parts

1.5 Seam allowance

Divide into 5 equal parts

Long side = 23.5

Short side = 15.5

Glue paper inside

Fold seam allowance and glue.

Bottom

Glue 2 pieces of paper

6cm

23.5 cm

15.5cm

Pincushion, shown on page 72.

MATERIALS
FABRICS: Off-white with pink flowers, pink with white small flowers, 45cm by 15cm each. Pink cotton broadcloth, 20cm by 17cm. Cotton jersey: Tomato red, 16cm by 8cm; green, 16cm by 10cm. Pink cotton tape, 2cm by 280cm. Peacock green felt. Cotton for stuffing.
FINISHED SIZE: See diagram.
DIRECTIONS:
1. Cut out strips from prints and sew strips and tapes together.
2. Weave tapes to make bottom of basket. Trim excess.

3. Bend tapes and continue to weave side.
4. Sew tape to top edges. Sew on handles.
5. Sew side seams of lining. Insert lining into basket. Turn in seam allowance and slip-stitch lining to basket.
6. Sew 2 pieces of tomato together with right sides facing leaving opening for stuffing. Turn inside out. Stuff with cotton and slip-stitch opening closed. Make avocado in same manner.
7. Sew stem and calyx to tomato.

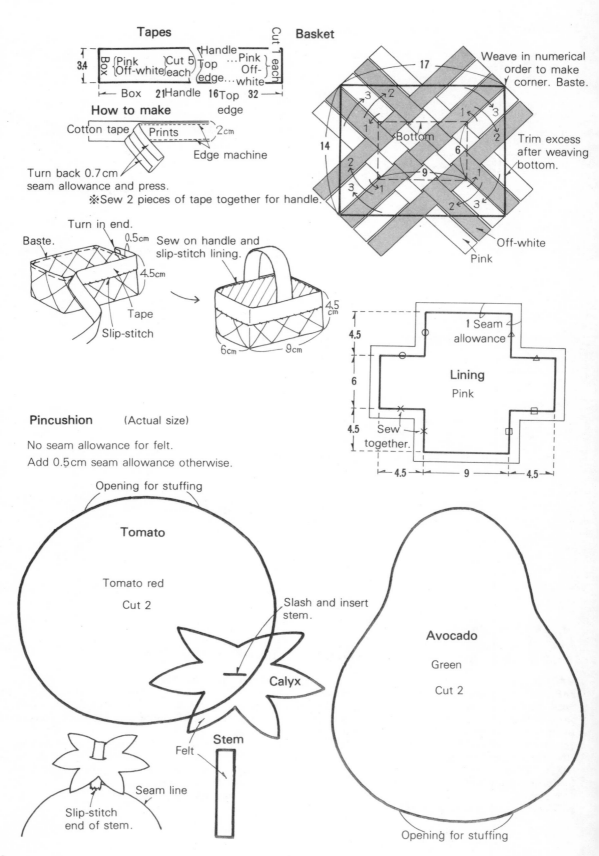

Tapes

Cut 1 each

Box 3.4

Pink
Off-white
} Box

Cut 5
each
} Handle
Top
edge

...Pink
...Off-white
} Top
edge

Box 21 Handle 16 Top 32

How to make

Cotton tape / Prints — 2cm

Edge machine

Turn back 0.7cm
seam allowance and press.
※Sew 2 pieces of tape together for handle.

Turn in end.
Baste. 0.5cm
Sew on handle and
slip-stitch lining.
4.5cm
Tape
Slip-stitch

4.5 cm
6cm 9cm

Basket

Weave in numerical
order to make
corner. Baste.

17

3 2
1 1 3
Bottom 2
14 6
2 1 9 1
3 1 2 3
2 3

Trim excess
after weaving
bottom.

Off-white
Pink

4.5

1 Seam
allowance

6

Lining

Pink

4.5
Sew
together.

4.5 9 4.5

Pincushion (Actual size)

No seam allowance for felt.
Add 0.5cm seam allowance otherwise.

Opening for stuffing

Tomato

Tomato red

Cut 2

Slash and insert
stem.

Calyx

Felt

Stem

Seam line

Slip-stitch
end of stem.

Avocado

Green

Cut 2

Opening for stuffing

MATERIALS

FABRIC: Sheeting: Peppermint green, 90 cm by 45 cm; mustard, 35 cm by 30 cm; cream and light orange, 23 cm by 18 cm each; pink 17 cm square. Quilt batting, 72 cm by 24 cm.

FINISHED SIZE: 72 cm by 23.5 cm. (Mat)

DIRECTIONS:

1. Sew 9 groups of 5 patches together by machine. Then join groups together.
2. Pin and baste top, batting and lining together. Quilt. Quilt Mat in same manner as Cover.
3. Appliqué telephone cord onto Cover. Bind edges to finish.

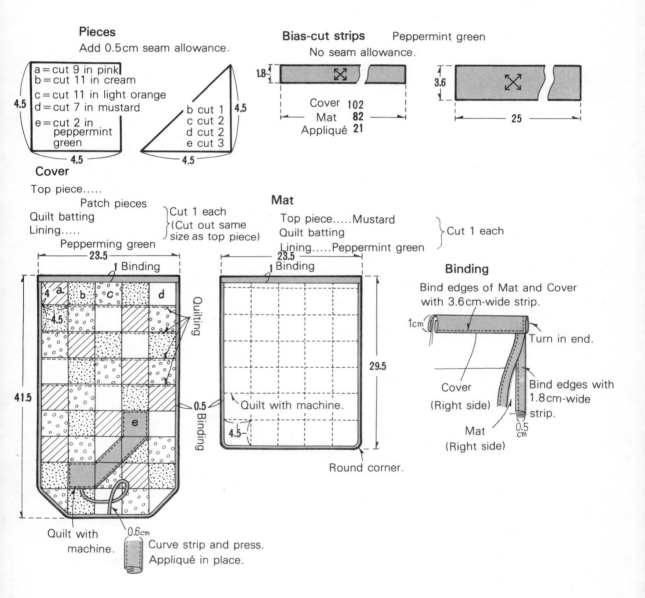

BASICS IN PATCHWORK

FABRIC: Many small pieces of fabric are sewn together to make patchwork; therefore, fabrics that are too thick, too thin, or that fray easily are not suitable. Medium weight cotton fabrics of plain weave are the most easily handled. New fabrics should be washed to pre-shrink them and remove starch. Press before use.

THREAD: To piece by hand, use cotton or mercerized thread, no. 30-50. If it is not available in colors that match the fabrics, silk thread or embroidery floss may be used. For machine sewing, use a thread that matches the fabric and the machine's gauge.

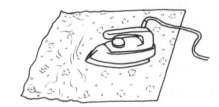

Cotton thread

Silk sewing thread

Embroidery thread

CUTTING: 1. Make actual-size patterns with cardboard or plastic sheet.

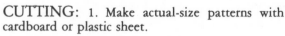

Cardboard or plastic sheet

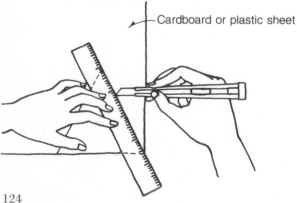

2. Place cardboard patterns on wrong side of fabric and trace around each pattern accurately, leaving a space twice as wide as seam allowance between patterns (about 1 cm—2 cm).
(Cutting pieces accurately is a must for a neat finish.)

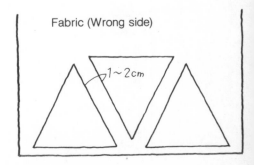

Fabric (Wrong side)

1~2 cm

PIECING: Method A (To piece by using cardboard templates)

This is the most traditional method to sew pieces together. Time and care must be required, but you may have a neater finish.

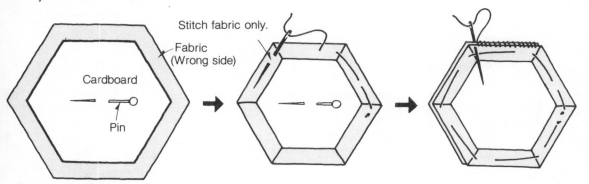

Make several templates with cardboard (or used postcards). Place template on wrong side of each patch piece and pin.

Turn seam allowances over template and baste, stitching through fabric only.

With right sides facing, overcast edges with tiny stitches.

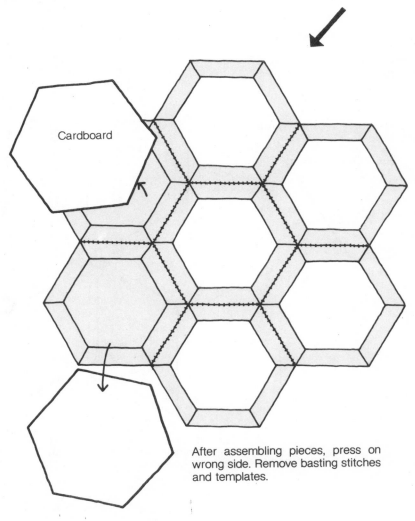

After assembling pieces, press on wrong side. Remove basting stitches and templates.

Method B (To piece by hand)

This is the easiest method for piecing straight seams.
Turn seams to one side.

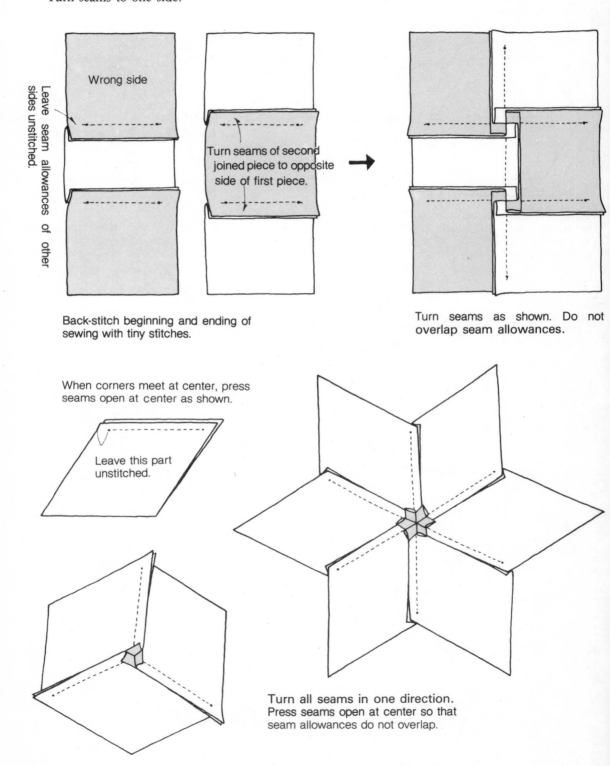

Leave seam allowances of other sides unstitched.

Wrong side

Turn seams of second joined piece to opposite side of first piece.

Back-stitch beginning and ending of sewing with tiny stitches.

Turn seams as shown. Do not overlap seam allowances.

When corners meet at center, press seams open at center as shown.

Leave this part unstitched.

Turn all seams in one direction. Press seams open at center so that seam allowances do not overlap.

Method C (To piece by machine)

Piecing by machine saves time, when you are making a big project. Seams are usually pressed open, but sometimes turned to one side.

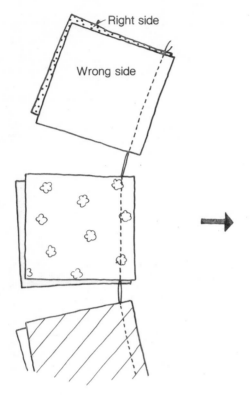

Sew one pair of pieces together by machine and continue to sew pairs of pieces without cutting thread.

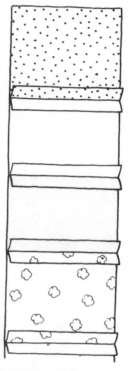

Cut thread between pairs and then sew pairs of pieces together.

QUILTING

Quilting is stitching two layers of top piece and lining together with padding between. Cotton and polyester quilt batting or flannel is used for padding. When you quilt by hand using running stitch, push the needle down through all the thicknesses, then push it up again at every stitch for a neater finish.

Movement of Needle

LINING FABRIC

Soft-finish cotton fabric of loose weave such as sheeting is more easily quilted than closely-woven cotton broadcloth.

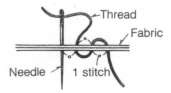

Push needle down vertically.

Place fabric on quilting pattern and trace, or trace the pattern using tracing paper and cellophane.

Fabric design
Tracing paper
Cellophane
Fabric

Top piece (Right side)
Interlining
Lining

Transfer quilting patterns to right side of top pieces, except pieces to be quilted along seams.
Draw straight lines directly on right side of top pieces with help of ruler.

Place quilt top, batting and lining together and baste three layers. Quilt along quilting lines.

QUILTING METHODS:

Quilt on seams (stitch in the ditch).

Quilt along seams.

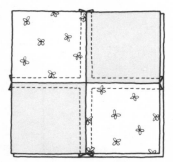

Quilt diagonally in two directions.

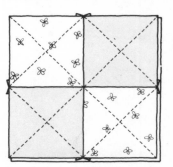

Quilt along quilting design.

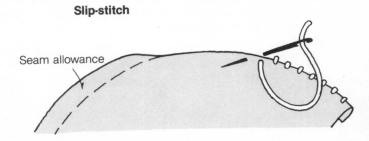

APPLIQUE

Slip-stitch

Seam allowance

Slip-stitch vertically, showing very little stitches.
(Turn in seam allowance at curves with help of needle as you sew.)